History's Greatest Generals: 10 Commanders Who Conquered Empires, Revolutionized Warfare, and Changed History Forever

By Michael Rank

Table of Contents

Introduction

Why Successful Generals are Black Sheep

If one wanted to name the worst place to find a good general, they could do far worse than the top of the military chain of command.

It is a strange statement to make, as generals are, by definition, career military men. They spend decades climbing the ranks and impressing their superior officers. No other obvious career path exists to become a commanding officer. Yet this has been true throughout history and was particularly true in the case of Confederate General Gideon Pillow. The man who has been described as "one of the most reprehensible men ever to wear the three stars and wreath of a Confederate general" by Steward Sifakis served as an officer for decades in the Army despite bungling nearly every attempt at military leadership. He was appointed Brigadier General of Volunteers in 1846 during the Mexican-American War due to being President James K. Polk's old law partner. He was successful in little but claiming other's accomplishments as his own. He took credit for American victories at Churubusco and Contreras by writing an anonymous letter to the New Orleans Delta and crediting himself for their success. His lie was discovered, and he was almost court-martialed by American commander Winfield Scott and Zachary Taylor. Polk intervened a second time to save his friend by having a paymaster claim responsibility for the letter.

After failing in bids for the U.S. Senate and the vice presidency, Pillow received another officer commission at the outbreak of the Civil War. Tennessee Governor Isham Harris made him a major-general in the state's provisional army. Although he was initially successful in such battles as the February 1862 assault at Fort Donelson, he pulled back his forces and squandered all of their hard-fought gains. He passed off his command to Simon Bolivar Buckner, who surrendered to Ulysses S. Grant. His successes dwindled after that point and devolved into outright cowardice. When he commanded a brigade at the January 2, 1863 Battle of Stones River, Pillow was found hiding behind a tree instead of leading his men. He was kept out of battle afterwards. After the war finished, he opened a law practice with the former Governor Harris.

Pillow's military career is infamous, but sadly it is a common story for generals throughout the ages. Great battle commanders and generals typically do not plan wars at the beginning of hostilities. They are usually well-connected members of the bureaucracy whose friends in high government positions give them command. Men like Pillow achieve these positions during times of peace when promotion depends on following rules and keeping to bureaucratic guidelines. They follow predictable, by-the-book strategies that rely on frontal attacks and direct assaults. It is for this reason that, sadly, Pillow thrived in the military profession. He was friends with the right people and predictable enough not to embarrass anyone important. He was also a by-the-numbers commander who did not take any risks and preferred direct attacks to the subterfuge of an attack on the enemy's flank.

Pillow may have been a bad general, but he fought in a way that was considered acceptable. Society favors direct solutions and personalities over novel or unfamiliar methods. This is true today as much as it was during the Civil War or World War II. Images of the Allied forces storming the beaches of Normandy and directly charging German gunners are looked upon with enormous admiration and respect. The commander who leads his soldiers head-on into battle is lionized and etched in military strategy. As a result, Bevin Alexander has noted that the U.S. Army equates war with American football. This sport consists of a direct challenge by an attack against a defender, and the two crash into each other to pound out every yard.

Such commanders are respected and follow orderly systems well, but they fare poorly when faced with an unpredictable enemy. In contrast, the great generals in history depended on surprise, deception, and subtlety. Alexander notes that practically all famous military maneuvers in history were made against the enemy's flank, whether real or psychological. Such an attack cuts off an enemy from his supplies, reinforcements, and communications. Weaker generals are psychologically undermined and quickly lose their confidence. A classic example of this strategy is Scipio Africanus, the Roman commander in the Second Punic War, who weakened Carthage's hold on Spain by ignoring its armies and attacking its main base in Cartagena. Napoleon was only defeated by the Allies in 1814 when they turned away from his army, not bothering with a direct attack, and captured Paris. This forced his people to surrender.

Another example of the unorthodox-but-successful general is the Byzantine commander Flavius Belisarius. He reconquered much of the Western Roman Empire in the sixth century after it had fallen to barbarians a century earlier. He did so by leading a small force of 5,000 soldiers against 10 times as many Goths and using brilliant and deceptive tactics. During the months-long siege of Naples in 537, he finally broke it by sending his soldiers through the aqueduct to bypass the city walls. They climbed down into the city center by means of an overhanging olive tree, quietly walked through the city to a tower in its wall, killed its defenders, and allowed their comrades in by throwing them rope ladders. They slaughtered the civilian population. When news of their victory spread, other Italian cities threw open their gates rather than suffer the same fate.

Belisarius then entered Rome and prepared for a long siege against a massive Gothic force. As the siege drug on and his army ran out of supplies, the general came up with an ingenious plan. He knew he could not lead his troops into a sortie, so he sent a subordinate officer to move north to Tuscany with 2,000 horsemen to raid Gothic towns. They found little resistance there because most Gothic men of fighting age were in Rome. Belisarius ordered him to advance to the Gothic capital of Ravenna. The Gothic commander Vittigis was so alarmed about the impending raid that he eventually withdrew. Belisarius had defeated them without a costly fight, and they swore their allegiance to Rome.

But like many other famous generals in history, Belisarius' unconventional nature and eccentricity earned him suspicion back home. He was not given a hero's welcome by the Byzantine Emperor Justinian, who considered him a political challenger. He earned the spite of the political leadership, who were deeply jealous of his success. He did not enjoy fame and renown back in Constantinople. Because great generals like Belisarius are outspoken and prone to individualism and self-promotion, they often live in infamy after their moments of glory. This is true even for those with fantastic success that saved the nation that they defended in battle. In 562 he stood trial in Constantinople on charges of corruption. He was found guilty and imprisoned, but the emperor later pardoned him. In the coda to Belisarius' life, legend has it that Justinian ordered his eyes to be put out, which reduced him to a homeless beggar near the Pincian Gate of Rome. He pled for alms from passers by before the emperor would pardon him.

This book will explore the lives and times of the 10 most successful generals in history. It will explore their unconventional and sometimes erratic behavior that brought them success but also made them black sheep. But before embarking on this survey, we must first determine what it means to be a successful commander. It is not as simple of a question as it appears.

Numerous factors determine the success of a commander; killing the highest amount of enemy soldiers is not sufficient criteria. Such a metric would inevitably bias this book in favor of modern generals with access to Hellfire missiles and satellite communications over ancient rulers that commanded the more primitive resources of infantry, archers, and cavalry. Instead it will examine characteristics that span space and time. First, the general must be an inspirational leader of his troops. He must be able to discipline them before entering battle and motivate them when circumstances appear desperate and defeat imminent. A successful general inspires these qualities in his troops through his personal virtue and bravery, not merely by giving a watered-down version of the St. Crispin's Day speech and watching the battle safely from his command tent. Such a general motivates his troops not only by courage on the battlefield, but also by quotidian aspects of being a good administrator. He must be able to handle the massive logistic effort of a war by keeping open supply lines for reinforcements, equipment, and weapons.

Second, a successful general must be an expert in strategy and tactics. Strategy is the art of long-term planning and foresight. It comes through gathering intelligence, choosing the manner of attack or defense, assessing the enemy's weaknesses, and manipulating rivalries. A truly successful commander executes a plan that avoids battle altogether and merely seeks victory. Napoleon did this time and time again, particularly with his deadly method of *manoeuvre sur les derrieres*: marching unexpectedly away from the enemy's main strength and concentrating on a weak but vital enemy point. He did this by securing a terrain feature in the rear such as a river and preventing the enemy from obtaining reinforcements or supplies. Tactics are the spur-of-the-moment, instinctual responses, the actual battle. They are the moments of improvisation that test a leader's creativity and flexibility. These come in the form of choosing when to give the order to attack, withdraw, or surrender. And a general must be able to execute his ingenuous plans on the ground for them to be effective. A sneak attack is easy to plan but difficult to carry out.

Finally, a successful general must produce results. First and foremost, they must be able to defeat their enemies in smaller skirmishes. Pillow is an excellent negative example of this principle. When Ulysses S. Grant fought Pillow at Fort Donelson, he knew that he could assault the fortress even without overwhelming superiority. This was a risky move according to the military calculus of the Civil War. But he had fought with Pillow in the Mexican-American War and knew of his milquetoast nature. Grant wrote in his memoirs that, "I had known General Pillow in Mexico, and judged that with any force, no matter how small, I could march up to within gunshot of any entrenchments he was given to hold." This is contrasted with Alexander the Great, who was undefeated in battle and broke the back of Persia, the most powerful empire at the time, not with superior numbers but never-before-seen battle maneuvers with his cavalry. In short, continual losses on the battlefield do not a famous commander make.

These victories are particularly notable because they came from a small force facing a larger opponent with superior technology. The battle of Thermopylae in 480 still lives in infamy, in which a force of 300 Spartans held back approximately one million soldiers of the Persian army for a week as the Athenian navy prepared a sea assault. If the commander is able to win the overall campaign, expand his territory, and increase his kingdom or nation's power, then he holds special commendation for success. The conquests of Genghis Khan and his immediate descendants stretched from the Pacific Ocean to Hungary. Napoleon threatened to conquer all of Europe when it had been politically fractured for nearly 2,000 years.

It is for these reasons that the generals in this book garner so much respect to this day, although less so in their lifetimes. Their battlefield strategies born of the era of spear and shield are still taught in military academies, even in the age of unmanned drones and guerrilla-style warfare. The names "Genghis" and "Alexander" are popular boy's names throughout the Muslim world, even though both were avowed pagans. They are the protagonists in thousands of books, films, plays, and video games.

So let us look at the lives of the 10 greatest generals in history, who through their ingenuity and indomitable spirit won wars, saved empires, and changed the course of history forever.

Chapter 1

Alexander the Great (356-323 B.C): From Irascible Macedonian Youth to World Conqueror

The mythology surrounding Alexander's life is so otherworldly that it might as well describe a Greek god. A prophetess declared him to be the son of Zeus rather than Philip of Macedon. According to Plutarch, his mother dreamed before consummating her marriage that her womb was struck by á thunder bolt, causing a flame to spread far and wide before dying out. The enormous Temple of Artemis in Ephesus burned down on the same day, due to the goddess herself being preoccupied with the warrior's emergence into the world. Other tales of his life say that Queen Thalestris of the Amazons brought 300 warrior maidens to Alexander as breed sows so that he might sire a super race.

Alexander even appears in the Bible and the Qur'an. In the book of Daniel, written 250 years before his birth, the Jewish prophet and Persian statesman describes him as a he-goat that "came from the west across the face of the whole earth, without touching the ground; and the goat had a conspicuous horn between his eyes." In the Qur'an he is described as a two-horned creature whom Allah had given great power, and he had traveled to the rising place and setting place of the sun. Here he built a wall to enclose Gog and Magog, which they will break out of on Judgement Day. Alexander would likely have been surprised that two monotheistic holy books complimented him so much, as he lived the immoral life of a drunken, pagan polytheist.

Nevertheless, his planet-sized reputation is well-earned. He was brilliant, well-educated, a great strategist, politically astute, extremely successful, and wise enough to appoint chroniclers to record his deeds. Alexander's reign began when he was 20 and ended at his death 13 years later. In that time, he conquered nations, expanded a fledgling empire to engulf much of the known world, and left a military legacy that overshadows the finest generals of all time. He not only showed the importance of battle strategy, but also the importance of logistics and politics in military campaigns. He may never have achieved his goal of becoming emperor of all Asia, but he led his army to conquest after conquest, making the Macedonian Empire into a military and economic power. The legacy of Alexander is a military primer that still teaches important lessons over two millennia later.

Alexander was born in 356 B.C. to King Philip II of the northern Greek kingdom of Macedon and his fourth wife, Queen Olympia. He grew in the shadow of his father's military career. On the day of his birth Philip was preparing a siege on the cit of Potidea on the peninsula of Chalcidice. Philip's military victories included the acquisition of Thrace and Northern Greece. Young Alexander was the beneficiary of these victories. His education consisted of lessons in the core areas of Macedonian refinement for the youth: riding, fighting, hunting, and literacy.

His powerful force of will exhibited itself even at a young age. When he was 10, Philip bought a horse from Thessaly that refused to be mounted. He thought it wild and ordered it away. According to Plutarch, Alexander understood that the horse merely feared its own shadow. Overcoming this problem, he tamed it quickly and named it Bucephalus, meaning "ox-head." His father beamed at his son's bravery and intelligence. He exclaimed, "My boy, you must find a kingdom big enough for your ambitions. Macedon is too small for you."

His ambitions made him a poor student, though. At the age of 13, Philip searched for a tutor for his hard-headed son. The irascible youth required an instructor who could reason with him and was not a simple autodidact. Philip found the answer in the magisterial scholar Aristotle, among the triumvirate of Western philosophy along with Socrates and Plato. He taught Alexander and the children of other

Macedonian nobles such as Ptolemy, Hephaistion, and Cassander, of whom many became his future generals and equally benefited from his course of instruction. Alexander proved to be an excellent student in philosophy, literature, and science. He loved the battle stories in the Odyssey and Ilaid. Aristotle gave him an annotated copy of the Iliad, and Alexander read it voraciously, always keeping it – and a short sword – underneath his pillow.

When he was 16, Alexander was appointed regent of Macedonia while Philip left on a campaign against Thrace. A group of Thracians from Maedi saw this as an opportunity to attack Macedonia directly while the king was in absentia. The young regent assembled an army and countered their offensive, defeating the invaders. They were ultimately driven from their territory, and their land was colonized with Greeks. He named the new settlement Alexandropolis.

Philip was pleased. He gave his son new responsibilities and dispatched Alexander with a small force to subdue revolts in the Thracian peninsula. At 18, Alexander was given command of a cavalry wing at the Battle of Chaeronea in which Macedon fought an alliance of Greek city-states, including Athens and Thebes. This was a revolt against Philip, who by then had become the de facto leader of Greece, and an abrogation against treaties signed with him. Alexander proved worthy of the appointment when his flank destroyed the Sacred Band of Thebans, the elite members of the Theban infantry. He was the first to break the ranks of the Sacred Bank, routed the troops, and ended the battle. The war of resistance against Philip came to an end. With no more internal opposition remaining, Philip turned his eyes eastward and prepared for total war against Greece's centuries-old enemy of Persia. He was voted supreme commander for a Panhellenic invasion. Philip would die before executing this long-awaited plan, but Alexander eagerly took up his mantle a few years later.

Under his father's tutelage, Alexander learned the advanced military strategy that allowed him to obtain such enormous conquests. Philip taught his soldiers to use the sarisa, a spear 16 feet long that allowed the phalanx formation to attack the enemy before they were within range of their opponent's infantry swords. Because these spears were not lightweight javelins, they required their wielder to use both hands. To defend the exposed spearmen, Philip created a class of shield bearers known as hypaspists. The formation itself was not sufficient to defeat an enemy core, but it did hold them in place; it acted as an anvil while the cavalry was used as the hammer to attack the enemy flanks. Each side of this phalanx core was flanked by cavalry units.

The Macedonian cavalry were known as the Companions and widely regarded as the best cavalry unit in the ancient world. They were the first shock cavalry in history as all others avoided direct melee into heavy combat. Each member rode the best horses and had the finest weaponry available. Each carried a xyston, a 12-foot-long thrusting spear, and wore a muscle cuirass, shoulder guards, and a Boeotian helmet. They were armed with a short sword for close combat. The Companions were organized into eight territorial squadrons numbering 200-300 cavalry. After the phalanx kept the enemy in place, the cavalry attacked from each side or attacked their rear guard. Alexander personally led the royal squadron of the Companion cavalry in the front of battle where he was easily recognizable. It made him a target, and he suffered many injuries due to this strategy, but it also inspired courage in his troops.

Macedon also had superior siege engines to complement its army. Bruce Upbin describes the unique form of siege warfare that Macedonian engineers developed to dominate their opponents defended by enormous city walls. It was a crucial innovation since earlier Greek armies lacked the ability to take such fortifications. The Spartans were never able to conquer Athens during the Peloponnesian War.

Central to their innovations in siege warfare was the siege tower. The tower had been in use by armies available since the 11th century B.C. in the ancient Near East, but he built an effective array of them. This allowed more men to be put on the walls than a simple ladder would allow. To this they added new forms of catapults and artillery that flung spears and missiles using fibers and tightly wound ropes as torsion devices. This powered two bow arms and allowed much greater force in their artillery. Their superior launch capabilities resulted in the creation of a large stone-throwing machine called the lithobolos, which could launch stones weighing up to 180 pounds (80 kg). This made breaching city walls a more important item in their conquest portfolio and helped the army avoid long sieges in which starvation conditions set in. Alexander used such artillery on the field as well as sieges.

In 336, Philip was assassinated. By this time, he had divorced Olympia, married Cleopatra Eurydice, and his relationship with Alexander had become tenuous. Alexander was no longer the guaranteed successor of his father. The tension between the two may have been born out of serious father-son rivalry, but it threatened to boil over. Plutarch captures a scene of their acrimonious relationship during Philip's wedding to Cleopatra: "At the wedding of Cleopatra... her uncle Attalus in his drink desired the Macedonians would implore the gods to give them a lawful successor to the kingdom by his niece. This so irritated Alexander, that, throwing one of the cups at his head, screamed, "You villain, what, am I then a bastard?" Then Philip, taking Attalus' part, rose up and would have run his son through, but by good fortune for them both, either his over-hasty rage, or the wine he had drunk, made his foot slip, so that he fell down on the floor. At which Alexander reproachfully insulted over him: "See there," said he, "the man who makes preparations to pass out of Europe into Asia, overturned in passing from one seat to another."

Alexander fled to Ilyria for fear of his life but returned six months later. By then the succession issue was resolved when Philip was assassinated by the captain of his bodyguards, Pausanias. The Macedonian nobles declared Alexander king at the age of 20. As the new ruler of Macedon, he was once again put to the test. Opportunistic rebels rose up against him when he ascended the throne, but he eliminated any potential rivals no matter his relation to them. Alexander killed close friends and even family members to secure his rule; it was a draconian but necessary measure in the fierce world of Greek politics. He executed his cousin Amyntas IV and two Macedonian princes from Lyncestis. In crushing domestic opposition to his rule, Alexander showed both skill and treachery. It was a skill likely learned from his mother, who in turn, killed Philip's new wife Cleopatra and her daughter Europa.

Alexander then turned his focus to those conquered territories attempting to secede from Macedonia. He quashed rebellions in Tribalia and Thrace, then rapidly deployed to Thebes to put down a Greek rebellion. He offered the Thebians a chance to surrender, but when they refused, he stormed the city, destroying almost every structure, killing 6,000, and putting 30,000 citizens into slavery. Other Greek cities considering rebellion quickly dropped their plans. Athens, Corinth, and Thermopylae swore their allegiance.

This early victory typified Alexander's battle tactics. Macedonia may have been a poor Greek state in the shadow of the Persian Empire, but it had a competent and professional military force that could quickly overwhelm most enemy armies. Alexander took this army and built it up to a war machine that would cross continents and obliterate everything in its path.

After consolidating his power, Alexander prepared to expand his father's legacy. Philip had died as he prepared for an invasion of Persia. The empire had harassed Greek states for centuries and threatened its total conquest on numerous occasions. Greek myths of heroic conquests in battle, primarily the battle of Thephanes in 480, speak of small Greek forces pushing back a massive Persian invasion force. Philip desired to launch an offensive strike and end the centuries of attacks that his kingdom had suffered from Persian emperors Cyrus to Darius III. Alexander consulted his father's advisors and began to prepare for a massive Eastern campaign. Many thought it would be a small surgical strike of key Persian fortresses and strongholds. His advisors never expected that he would launch a multi-decade campaign across the known world. He heeded the words of his tutor Aristotle to unite East and West.

Upon the safeguarding his northern borders, he prepared his crossing into Asia with 50,000 soldiers, 6,000 cavalry, and a fleet of 120 ships with almost 40,000 crew members. He deployed forces quickly, giving his opponents little chance to prepare. His army formation included heavily armed and skilled soldiers in front who were pushed from behind by supporting troops. The front soldiers were known as phalaiazn, and were equipped with sarissaes. The army flanks included archers, slingers, and cavalry.

As they began their Asia campaign, Alexander inspired his troops through personal bravery to lead them in front of battle, a commitment to victory, and respect toward fallen soldiers. When his army arrived in Asia by crossing the Hellespont, he thrust his spear into Anatolian soil to claim the continent as a gift from the gods. Alexander gave due respect to those who fell in battle. Although imagining himself to be divine, he did not treat the lives of his soldiers as an invaluable commodity. If they died in battle, he exempted their families from taxation and public service. Notable persons were commemorated with statues.

Alexander was also known as a wise general off the battlefield. He made the effort to visit with and fraternize with his soldiers, which inspired loyalty in battle. He dressed in the same uniforms as his subordinates. Soldiers received meager pay, but Alexander ensured that they received booty after each conquest (a commission-based payment system that incentivized soldiers to fight for over a decade in an alien land in order to plunder its riches). He was an expert logistician and ensured that his army was well-fed and properly equipped. This is an often mitigated part of his success, but it was as boring as it is essential. History is littered with armies defeated not by their enemies, but rather by their empty stomachs or lack of equipment.

His first Persian victory was at the Battle of the Granicus in 334 B.C. His army was smaller but more skilled than his opponents' and he won despite the presence of reluctant Greeks within his ranks. He let loose the horse companions in their wedge-shaped charge and crushed the center of the Persian line. The cavalry then routed the Persian infantry.

Following this battle Alexander accepted the surrender of Sardis, a Persian provincial capital. His army proceeded along the Aegean coast, laying siege to many cities starting with Halicarnassus. From there he moved into the mountains of Lycia and onto the Pamphylian plain. He eliminated Persian naval bases, cutting to pieces their supply chain in Asia Minor. He then moved inland to Termessos. When he arrived at the Phrygian city of Gordium, it is here that narratives of his life confirm his inevitably great destiny. According to an oracle, whoever undid the intractable knot of cornel bark would become the king of all Asia. When he couldn't find the end of the knot in its endless entanglement, he simply sliced it in half with his sword. This pragmatic approach to enigmatic problems is known as the "Alexandrian solution."

At Issus in northern Syria, Alexander first encountered the army of Darius III. It was easily defeated, which terrified the Persian emperor, as his army outnumbered the Macedonians two-to-one. In victory, Alexander's troops killed tens of thousands. Darius fled the battlefield and left behind his mother, wife, and two daughters. He attempted to ransom them for 10,000 talents and offered Alexander all the lands that he had previously won in Anatolia. The Macedonian refused. According to the chroniclers, Darius' mother Sisygambis took revenge on his cowardice by denouncing him and adopting Alexander as her own. For his part, Alexander was magnanimous in victory to Sisygambis and the rest of Darius' family. However, he rejected the emperor's even more generous terms of surrender following the siege of Tyre. The emperor offered him 30,000 talents for his family, to marry his eldest daughter, and all the land east of the Euphrates River. When Alexander still refused due to his mission to conquer, it put fear in nearby barbarian nations. Most simply swore their allegiance rather than face him on the battlefield.

Alexander could be churlish to his vanquished foes, but the kindness that he extended to Sisygambis was not an anomaly. He often treated his opponents with respect and even kindness. But at other times, he could be ruthless in his use of mass executions or enslavement. What explains this dichotomy? It was not due to an erratic or mercurial temper. Most likely, it demonstrated Alexander's brilliant political abilities. At times a fierce disposition that commanded respect, obedience, and loyalty were necessary to lead an army of thousands into unknown lands on a different continent. Alexander may have allowed his troops to massacre all the men of a city and enslave all the women and children, as he did in Tyre in 332 B.C., but they knew that a similar wrath could befall them if they did not follow orders. Ransacking, pillaging, and slaughtering an entire city also sent a message to the next potential enemy. Whether alliance or annihilation, the action depended on Alexander's current strategy.

This approach could be seen during Alexander's continued conquest of the Phoenician coast. When he reached the island of Tyre, the citizens refused to surrender. Alexander laid siege to the city for next seven months. Unable to launch an attack by sea, Alexander expended a great deal of resources to build a causeway. When Tyre finally surrendered, he destroyed the city, killing 7,000 people and enslaving 30,000. He reserved his mercy for the King of Tyre and his family. He then moved on to Gaza, where the citizens surrendered following a two-month siege.

In Egypt he once again demonstrated his deft political skills. He charmed the theocracy's political elite by undertaking a religious pilgrimage and endearing himself to the priests at the oracle. In 331 B.C., Alexander entered Egypt where he was greeted as a liberator after two centuries of Persian rule. He combined this victory with the strategic decision to build a city at the mouth of the River Nile. This city was designed as a strategic naval and commercial port. It was named Alexandria in his honor; decades later his general Ptolemy made it the capital of his empire, and it became the center of scientific inquiry in the ancient world. Alexander also made a pilgrimage to the temple and oracle of Amon-Ra. She was the Egyptian sun god and connected with the Macedonian deity Zeus Ammon. The priests at the temple declared Alexander to be the son of Zeus Ammon, just as the pharaohs had been declared the sons of Amon-Ra.

After conquering Egypt, Alexander returned to Tyre for a final battle with Darius. The once-revered god king had been pushed closer to *terra firma* with his military losses. Alexander had captured Susa and the ceremonial capital of Persepolis, which was burned as revenge for the burning of the Athenian Acropolis during the Second Persian War. Darius fled through Media and Parthia. He was eventually imprisoned by the satrap Bessus, who stabbed him. At his death, the Achaemenid Empire fell and Persia came under Greek rule. Alexander sought to kill Bessus as a usurper, and his campaign chased him throughout Central Asia. He was caught and executed in 329 B.C., but not before Alexander founded cities throughout the region, such as modern-day Kandahar in Afghanistan and Eschate in Tajikistan.

Alexander did not force the Persians into assimilating into Macedonian or Greek culture. Quite the opposite; he assumed Persian garb, ceremonial titles, customs, and court culture. In particular he adopted rituals of respect that Persians showed their superiors, such as specific forms of prostration and symbolic kissing of the hand. Alexander maintained a flexible policy of absorbing the resources and customs of conquered lands into his military force and leaving locals in charge of the nascent districts that he left in his wake of conquest. This was actually quite a common governing strategy in the ancient world; allowing a native son to rule a region was a far better deterrent to rebellion than installing a foreign figure. He appointed Persians as provincial governors and encouraged the recruitment of Persian troops into his forces. He compelled his soldiers to take Persian brides. The strategy of weaving the two cultures together would, over time, mitigate the possibility of war or rebellion. It was a pragmatic means of uniting two states that had warred with each other for centuries and did not share a language, legal code, or pantheon of gods.

Yet Alexander was not universally loved by his soldiers during the campaign, particularly for his tendency to appropriate foreign culture. Alexander believed in realpolitik, but many of his Macedonian soldiers saw him otherwise as an opportunist who lacked principles. While he was winning an empire, he was losing at home. A number of his officers believed he had forsaken his Macedonian lineage. By taking on Persian ceremony, his kinsman believed that he claimed respect for himself reserved solely for the gods. It is important to remember that Alexander's troops most likely did not believe him to be divine during his lifetime; myths of his contemporaries thinking him the son of Zeus only sprang up after his death.

A plot against Alexander to overthrow him was revealed. Philotas, the commander of the cavalry, was tried and executed as the leader of the coup attempt. Alexander then demanded the execution of his father, Parmenio, to prevent him from taking vengeance upon him and engineering a second coup. It was a bold move, as Parmenio was a respected general, and his execution was deeply unpopular with the rank-and-file. Those around Alexander increasingly feared his temper and found his behavior to be erratic.

Alexander entered matrimony more than once in the campaign, but it was done primarily to secure alliances. In 327 B.C., he married Roxanne, a Bactrian princess and one of his three wives. It was his only marriage of love; he married Stateira II, daughter of Darius, and Parysatis II of Susa, for political reasons. The following year, his army marched to Punjab to extend his empire east of Persia.

When Alexander's army was on the march, it resembled a mobile city more than a modern-day military force. Some troops traveled with their wives and children, or at least the slave concubines that they acquired along the campaign. Many non-essential personnel were in tow. Alexander traveled with engineers, poets, historians, scientists, doctors, slave traders, and his chronicler - which explains the copious records of his campaign left behind to history. He established a supply chain with conquered states to provide the necessary materials for his army. However, they were often required to live off the land and trade with towns and cities through which they passed due to the decade-long length of their campaign.

Alexander reached the eastern edge of his campaign

when he encountered Pakistani chieftains and called upon them to submit to his authority. In 327/326 B.C. he led a campaign against those who refused. He destroyed the clans of Aspasioi, Guraean, and Assakenoi, but not without suffering injuries in his shoulder and ankle. He then crossed the Indus River and waged war against the Punjabi ruler King Poras in the famous Battle of the Hydaspes.

Alexander's pre-battle maneuvers are considered his most brilliant use of battle tactics. He and his force had to cross the Jhelum River. It was deep and fast enough to carry away an attacking force that attempted to cross it, as Porus was set up on the south bank to repel any crossing. Alexander took a small force of 6,000 troops upstream and crossed the river in secrecy through manufacturing "skin floats filled with hay." He shocked the Punjabi king with his force, which crossed the river despite all reasonable expectation.

To make the battle among the most surreal in history, Alexander's troops commenced battle during a thunderstorm and faced what no European-based land force had ever encountered before: infantry flanked by war elephants. The elephants stormed their lines and caused significant harm to the Macedonian phalanx. They were eventually able to gather their wits and repulse them with their spears. The phallangitai locked their shields and pressed on their enemy. In the end, approximately 1,000 of Alexander's men died versus 23,000 Indians. The conquest turned the Punjab into a Macedonian satrap and opened India to Hellenistic political and cultural influence.

It is here that the domains of Alexander reached their maximum extent. The breadth of his conquests enveloped over two dozen modern-day nations and every major culture from Greece to Egypt, Persia, India, and everything in between. Plutarch's famous phrase was made here when he said that, "When Alexander saw the breadth of his domain, he wept, for there were no more worlds to conquer" – a quote perhaps better immortalized by the erudite villain Hans Gruber in "Die Hard."

Alexander wanted to continue eastward, but his troops

began to revolt, voicing concern over Indian reinforcements of troops and supplies. They were exhausted by years of campaigning and longed to see their families again. Reluctantly, Alexander agreed. The Macedonian army decided to return home by moving south along the Hydaspes and Indus Rivers. They constructed a navy of 1,000 ships and floated them along the rivers to ferry supplies. At Malli, the troops met strong resistance amongst the local clans. Alexander was badly wounded with a spear to the chest. Despite his injury, the troops fought on to victory. Alexander recovered and the campaign continued.

After the Indian campaign, Alexander made controversial pronouncements that risked further factionalism in the army. He sent part of his army to southern Iran along with the fleet to explore the Persian Gulf. The rest traveled through the Gedrosian Desert and Makran, but not before many died in the arid climate. The dislike for his marching orders was surpassed only by his plans to merge Hellenistic with Persian culture. In keeping with his goal to unify the empire, he legitimized the marriages of his soldiers to Persian women. He relieved 10,000 Macedonian soldiers of duty and sent the elderly and disabled veterans back to Macedon, but only after he had incorporated 30,000 Persians into his army. Alexander said this decision was intended to give rest for his weary soldiers, but his dissenters interpreted the command as an attempt to mitigate the Macedonia character of the army. He arrested 13 of the leaders who had condemned his Persian troops and manners and executed them.

Near the end of his life, Alexander traveled to Ecbatana to retrieve the Persian treasury. In 324 his friend (and possibly lover) Hephaestion died from fever. It was a stunning blow to the young emperor. The two shared unyielding bonds. His death is touch upon significantly by the ancient sources due to the effects that it had on Alexander. Chroniclers claim that he commanded extensive and extreme signs of mourning among his army, such as the tails of all horses be shorn and the banning of flutes and all forms of music. He refused to eat or drink for days and was thrown into extreme grief. The cost of Hephaestion's funeral was estimated at 12,000 talents, which some estimate to be the equivalent of $2 billion today. An enormous pyre 60 meters high was designed by the famous artist Stasicraetes and built in stepped levels. It was adorned with gold and ornately details with scenes of Greek mythology.

Following his friend's death, Alexander entertained admiral Nearchus and enjoyed a session of heavy drinking with Medius of Larissa, partly for diplomacy, but partly to assuage his grief. This resulted in a nasty bout of fever. It grew until he was unable to speak for the next two weeks. Alexander died shortly after in 323 BC at the age of 32 at the palace of Nebuchadnezzar II in Babylon.

For all his planning and success, Alexander had given insufficient thought to succession. He had no legitimate heir as his son Alexander IV was born after his death. One account said that he gave detailed instructions to his general Craterus for further commands after his death. They included conquest of the western Mediterranean, circumnavigation of Africa, transplanting populations from Asia to Europe and Europe to Asia to interbreed his subject class, and to build a monument to his father Philip that would match the greatest in all of Egypt.

These orders were ignored by his generals. They fought each other for succession for the next 40 years and established a number of daughter kingdoms. It was a quick end to the meteoric rise of the Macedonian Empire, but despite the schism, four empires were born, all with clear Greco-Macedonian roots. They were the Ptolemaic Kingdoms of Egypt, the Seleucid Empire in Persia, the Kingdom of Pergamom in Asia Minor, and Macedon.

The lessons of Alexander to military generals today are numerous, and they are still taught in military academies. Treat soldiers with respect, keep supply lines strong, create a well-disciplined army with strategic troop formations, and know when to resort to diplomacy and when to resort to battle. He regarded his soldiers highly, frequently walking through the camp and stopping to talk and listen to groups of men. He allowed them to take booty in conquest, which motivated them to win battles. But he dealt ruthlessly with those guilty of betrayal and frequently executed suspects in coup attempts.

Furthermore, Alexander was sensitive to cultural differences and capable of ruling subject classes of enormously different backgrounds. He showed deference to foreign customs and introduced them into his own court. He could win over administrators, religious leaders, and feign interest in foreign gods. He did so all while making sure that Macedonians remained in control.

He was beloved far and wide in the coming decades and centuries, particularly by military commanders. In 63 B.C., a young Roman quaestor in Spain approached a statue of Alexander to pay homage to the commander, who had never lost a battle in his remarkable career. He broke down and wept before it. The 30-year-old realized that the Macedonian already conquered the world at his age, while he was a mere administrator in a backwater Roman province who had frittered away his youth. The stone face smiled back at him, satisfied in his reputation as a military colossus.

This young man, Julius Caesar, eventually found his bearings and went on to his own successful career of conquest. He would raise up his own empire and lead armies to extraordinary victory. But it was to Alexander whom his knee bent, perhaps the only human worthy of such an act of praise by a Caesar.

Chapter 2

Hannibal of Carthage (247-182 B.C.): The Father of Strategy and the Bane of the Roman Republic

The most feared enemy of ancient Rome grew up in a culture of death. Hannibal Barca, whose name in Punic meant "Baal is merciful to me," was raised as a worshipper of the ancient Canaanite god that demanded child sacrifice in order to be appeased. When he was seven, Hannibal stood at the edge of a sacrificial fire pit and witnessed his parents hand over his infant sibling to a priest. The robed figured held him before a bronze idol in raised arms. He slit the throat of the child, causing quick death, and placed the body on the outstretched hands of the statue. It remained there for a few moments before sliding into the pyre.

Hannibal's father, Hamilcar Barca, was a Carthaginian commander and leader in the Mercenary War and the Punic conquest of Iberia. He raised his son in the customs of the deeply religious society, founded in 814 B.C. as a Phoenician trading colony. Baal worship was as brutal in the North African society as it had been 1,000 years earlier, when Canaanites slaughtered children by the thousand, much to the horror of the ancient Israelites. It was an abominable practice, even by the standards of the late Bronze Age; so much so that in the Old Testament, God ordered Israel's army to completely destroy the civilization of the Baal worshippers upon their entrance into the Holy Land.

The practice, however, continued to thrive in Hannibal's lifetime. Cleitarchus wrote in the third century B.C. that Carthaginian families promised at least one of their children to their gods in order to obtain favor. Plutarch notes that childless couples would purchase children from destitute families as a substitution. Contemporary Romans and Greeks found the practice equally barbaric. They regarded it as proof enough that the society deserved to be conquered, subdued, and, if need be, destroyed.

Unlike Rome's neighbors in Iberia and Gaul, the task of conquering Carthage would not be made simple. Under the direction of the brilliant tactician Hannibal, it represented the greatest existential threat to the young Roman Republic.

He came of age when Mediterranean powers scrambled to gain supremacy over its neighboring states due to a power vacuum in the region. Carthage contended with Rome, Syracuse, and the deteriorating daughter states of Alexander's former empire – Macedon, the Seleucid Empire, and Ptolemaic Egypt. Hannibal certainly had the intelligence and determination to make his North African city-state the pre-eminent state in the ancient world. He even appeared destined to this result in his early military victories, particularly the battle of Cannae, which threatened to undo the Roman Republic.

Yet, for all his successes on the battlefield, Hannibal was unable to achieve final victory over the other claimants to Mediterranean supremacy. This is due chiefly to his inability to win the long game of the Second Punic War despite his success at the short game. Furthermore, for all his grand strategy, he failed as a statesman to convert these military victories into political capital and win the Carthaginian aristocracy to his side. Nonetheless, his strategies were so innovative that he is frequently named in the pantheon of antiquity's greatest generals, along with Alexander the Great, Scipio Africanus, Julius Caesar, and Pyrrhus of Epirus. He is a patron saint to modern-era strategists, such as Napoleon Bonaparte.

Hannibal's legacy is also irreparably distorted due to the biased sources that survive him. No historical accounts of his life survived the Third Punic War and the Roman destruction of Carthage. None of his countrymen left any account of his life, nor did panegyrics or songs of his military brilliance survive. All that remain are accounts by Roman chroniclers, who were employed to present him as the enemy of civilization. As a result, they depicted his life and times in the most negative manner possible. Of 37 authors that mention him, not a single comment is positive. Yet they had to accede that he was a tactician extraordinaire, even if this was to emphasize that his final defeat made Rome's ascendancy all the more glorious.

Hannibal was born in 247 B.C. His father Hamilcar had led the Carthaginians at the end of the First Punic War with Rome. The war ended when Hamilcar surrendered Sicily to Rome and peace was negotiated. Not resting for a moment, he quickly set out to improve the fortunes of his state and fix its dismal financial condition. Hamilcar first subjugated the tribes of the Iberian Peninsula in order to extract tribute. It was not a simple task to accomplish due to their penury. The Carthaginian navy was so strapped for resources after its war with Rome that the troops could not be transported by ship all the way to Iberia; rather, they were marched to the Pillars of Hercules and crossed into Europe by being transported across the Strait of Gibraltar. He took his young son on this campaign, but only under the condition that swear never to be a friend of Rome.

At home Carthage remained in a tenuous situation. It struggled to quell an uprising among its former mercenaries who had not received proper compensation for their services. Rome took advantage of the disarray by capturing the Carthaginian islands of Sardinia and Corsica. Its eye was on territorial expansion at the expense of its enemy.

Hamilcar died in 229 B.C. by drowning in battle during the conquest of Hispania. He was succeeded by his son-in-law Hasdrubal, who preferred accommodation to Rome instead of aggression. He consolidated Carthage's Iberian holdings and signed a treaty with Rome that stated he would not expand north of the Ebro River as long as Rome did not expand beyond its south.

The treaty was merely an armistice. Hasdrubal worked quietly behind the scenes to shore up his support on the European continent and raise up a massive army to attack Rome. He arranged a marriage between Hannibal and the Iberian princess Imilce. He himself was a sharp tactician, and prepared the overland campaign to Italy that Hannibal would execute years later. But none of his plans came to fruition, as he was assassinated in 221 BC. Hannibal was appointed to succeed him at the age of 26.

The young commander-in-chief quickly returned to his father's aggressive military approach. He inaugurated this strategy by completing the conquest of Hispania through the capture of military fortifications and garrisons. In his first campaign he stormed the Olcades' strongest center, Alithia. He then captured the Vaccaei strongholds of Helmantice and Arbucala. Rome, fearful of his growing strength, allied with the city of Saguntum, which lay south of the River Ebro. Hannibal considered this a breach of the treaty signed after the First Punic War. He pressed on with the siege and captured Saguntum after eight months before turning his gaze toward Italy.

The capture of Saguntum sat poorly with the Romans. They demanded his extradition for violation of the treaty. Hannibal, however, did not prefer to idly await a fate of incarceration, deportation to Rome, torture, and death. He consolidated his family's hold on power and appointed his brother, also named Hasdrubal, as commander. He crossed the river Ebro, and the Second Punic War with Rome officially began.

Hannibal desired to carry the war through Hispania and Gaul into central Italy. His foes expected an easy defeat against a small city-state punching above its military weight. They did not expect a protracted battle against heretofore unforeseen military tactics and a long war of attrition.

One of the first strategies that general enacted was to not directly attack the strongest position of his opponent. Therefore, while Rome prepared for a Carthaginian attack on Sicily, Hannibal was determined not to repeat the mistakes of the First Punic War. He prepared an attack on Italy overland from the mountainous north via a high-altitude and precarious path. He departed Carthage in 218 BC.

Hannibal marched across the Pyrenees with 38,000 infantry, 8,000 cavalry, and 37 elephants. Despite an early fall snow, Hannibal's massive army moved quickly, ferrying the elephants across the Rhone River and then crossing the Alps. It was an enormously risky maneuver that exposed his

25

force to death by cold, starvation, or attack by blocked passages. Only half of Hannibal's forces that entered Italy survived the march. Nevertheless, Livy writes that he led the mountain crossing with ingenuity in the face of seemingly intractable problems. According to a Roman's account, he used vinegar and fire to break through a rockfall. The gamble eventually paid off, as the Romans could not take any measures to halt his advance through Gaul. Hannibal secured conciliation from Gaullish chiefs along his passage and prepared for an attack on Italy.

The Roman consul Publius Cornelius Scipio was sent to intercept his forces, but his commanders wrongly assumed he would enter Europe via Iberia. He intercepted Hannibal with a small detachment from Gaul upon hearing of his mountain crossing. They clashed at Ticinius at the Battle of Trebia, where Hannibal won a decisive victory using his superior cavalry forces. The results of the battle were devastating for the Romans: Scipio was badly injured, and they had to abandon the Lombardi plains. States recently absorbed into the Roman Republic – the Gauls and Ligurians – swore allegiance to Hannibal's nascent European state, which fortified his depleted troop strength. Rome ordered a force led by Tiberius Sempronius Longus to bring his army back from Sicily and join up with the army of Scipio Africanus, the son of Publius Cornelius Scipio, to face Hannibal.

Although Hannibal was unable to stop Sempronius and Scipio's armies from uniting, he could capitalize on the generals' discordant methods of attack. While Sempronius assumed command over the more experienced Scipio, Hannibal planned his attack. He sent 2,000 soldiers led by his brother Mago in the cover of darkness to flank the Roman's encampment and lie in wait for the battle. He then organized an attack for the next day. Using a strategy that he would employ again and again in subsequent encounters, he placed his strongest troops on the flank, knowing that his enemy would attack that point.

Dawn arrived, and he sent a small cavalry force to entice the Romans to attack. When they took the bait, he was ready.

The Romans used the standard three-column formation, flanked by cavalry. Eventually, the weaker Roman flanks started to fail, at which point Mago's troops attacked and crushed the remaining resistance while Hannibal's troops pursued them. It is estimated that the Romans lost as many as 20,000 troops.

After their defeat at Trebia, the Romans brought in new leadership to challenge Hannibal, whom they realized had been dangerously underestimated. Gaius Flaminius replaced Sempronius. After a difficult crossing through marshlands in central Italy, he arrived in Etruria in the spring of 217 B.C. Hannibal rampaged through the countryside and harassing villagers in an attempt to lure the Romans into another battle. He expected to play on Flaminius' fear of popular reproach for passivity. When he refused to engage him, Hannibal cut off the Roman troops from their supply lines to Rome. At this point, the Roman Senate demanded action. Flaminius prepared for battle near Lake Trasimene, where Hannibal set up his troops for an ambush. A narrow gorge was the only access to a small plain near the lake. Hannibal exposed his troops to the enemy near the gorge to entice the Romans to attack and positioned his heavy infantry while hiding his light infantry.

Further to the west, he positioned his cavalry and additional troops in order to intercept a Roman retreat. To further confuse the Romans, he had camp fires lit in the unoccupied Touro Hills. Flaminius arrived, ready to attack before his troops, commanded by Gnaeus Servilius Geminus, had joined his force. His impatience was rewarded in kind. Hannibal attacked with a small force that split Flaminius' front troops from the main army, then attacking them with his troops that had been waiting in the hills. The Romans fought gallantly but were unable to mount an effective counterattack. Their westernmost troops were forced into the lake, the majority of the infantry was defeated, and the rest retreated. Over half the 25,000 Roman soldiers were killed. Hannibal's maneuver, in which he marched around his opponent's left flank, was the first recorded turning movement in military history. Flaminius was killed, making this the worst ambush in Roman military history until the Battle of Carrhae against the Parthinians.

After this disastrous defeat, Rome finally began to take the threat of the Carthaginian general seriously. The only force that could prevent Hannibal's advance on Rome had been destroyed. The Senate appointed Quintus Fabius Maximus as dictator with complete executive control to counter Hannibal's assault on the Italian peninsula. Fabian himself was a shrewd tactician and preferred cunning over a direct military assault on the powerful Carthaginian army. He crafted a strategy to exploit his opponent's two principal weaknesses. First, Hannibal had weak supply lines from Carthage to Italy; resupply depended on enlisting the support of Rome's enemies to sell weapons, clothing, siege equipment, and other essential provisions. Second, his army mainly consisted of mercenaries from Gaul and Spain that hated Rome more than they loved Carthage. They were suitable for direct, pitched battle but not for long sieges that required patience and the equipment that they lacked.

Fabius exploited these two disadvantages. He refused to directly engage the Carthaginian and forced him into a war of attrition. The general sent out small detachments against Hannibal's foraging parties but never faced him in pitched battle. He dispatched several Roman armies in Hannibal's vicinity to limit his movements. Fabius led Hannibal into Italy's hilly terrain, nullifying the advantage of his cavalry. Villagers were instructed to flee into fortified towns and bring their livestock and possessions upon sight of the Carthaginian army, depriving them of supplies or plunder. In this protracted war, Hannibal continued his trek down to the Southeastern corner of Italy, attacking towns, cutting off supply lines, and gaining control of the supply depot at Cannae. He ravaged Apulia and marched through the rich and fertile provinces of Samniun and Campania. But much to his dismay, he could not strike a fierce blow against the Roman army.

Fabius' strategy was initially successful, but it infuriated the Roman rank-and-file as a cowardly strategy. Older senators supported the campaign, but officers and soldiers considered it unbecoming of an army accustomed to crushing its enemies directly on the battlefield. Although it deprived Carthage of victory and stretched its forces thin, the strategy ultimately failed due to lack of support from the army. They were infuriated that Hannibal plundered Italy unopposed. Marcius Minucius Rufus, a political enemy of Fabius, was quoted as saying, "Did we come here to see our allies butchered, and their property burned, as a spectacle to be enjoyed? And if we are not moved with shame on account of any others, are we not on account of these citizens... a Carthaginian foreigner, who was advanced even this far from the remotest limits of the world, through our dilatoriness and inactivity?"

In 216 B.C. the Senate replaced him with the Roman consuls Gaius Terentius Varro and Lucius Aemilius Paullus and raised up an enormous army of 50-80,000 men. They readied for battle at Cannae along the Aufidus River. Their plan was to attack with a strong, tight infantry at the center, which was flanked by the cavalry. Hannibal had set up his army with light infantry flanked by experienced infantry and cavalry. When the battle began, the Carthage forces surged forward, pushing back the Roman troops in what looked like a crescent. The cavalry on the left flank made quick work of their enemies and swung around to the rear of the Romans to assist their counterparts on the right flank. Hannibal then had his central infantry retreat slowly while those on the outside held their ground. Upon his order, they surged along with the flanking cavalry.

This maneuver, known as the double envelopment maneuver, is considered by most military historians to be Hannibal's masterpiece. It is a way for an inferior force to defeat a superior force on open terrain. The larger army advances to the center of the smaller army, which responds by moving its outside forces to the enemy flanks to surround it. Once the larger army is dispersed, a second layer of pinchers attacks on its more extreme flanks to prevent reinforcements. However, it is enormously difficult to execute, since it requires well-trained cavalry to successfully deploy the complex maneuver. Furthermore, the battlefield commander must have intimate knowledge of the battlefield terrain, since any unknown feature of the landscape can leave him open to surprises from the enemy, which will disrupt the complex sequence of events that makes for a successfully double envelopment.

Hannibal executed the maneuver successfully, and the Romans were surrounded. He had severed their Achilles tendon. Despite having inferior numbers, he obliterated their forces. Over 50,000 troops were killed and 5,000 taken prisoner. Among the dead were three consuls, the quaestors, and 80 out of the Roman Republics 300 senators. It was such an enormously psychological blow to Rome, as well as a physical one. Rome had lost one-fifth of its population of males over 17 years of age due to this battle and three other campaign seasons.

Hannibal's victories in battle brought many of Italian city-states to his side. But these new vassals did not provide him with sufficient troops or constitute a sufficient supply chain. Problems of fighting a war on foreign soil that had plagued his campaign since the beginning had not disappeared. Hannibal still lacked the resources to lay siege to Rome, an exceptionally well-fortified city that would take several months to capture. This was true even though he had captured Italy's second largest city, Capua, which he had made into his base. Hannibal found his new Italian allies less than willing to fight and, at the same time, Carthage's leadership offered him little support. Maharbal, the commander of the Numidian cavalry, commented on his predicament that, "Hannibal, you know how to gain a victory, but not how to use one."

The diminishing fortunes of Hannibal's Italian campaign and a strategic stalemate with Rome pointed to an inevitable conclusion. He was a superior general but still lacked the resources to conquer his enemy. By then Rome had adjusted accordingly. The Senate and army begrudgingly admitted the effectiveness of Fabius' strategy of retreat and called for its implementation. By leading Hannibal through a second war of attrition, Rome was able to regain control of Capua in 211 BC and then Syracuse after laying siege. He still won victories, such as the destruction of two Roman armies in 212 B.C. and killing two consuls in a 208 battle. But his Italian allies inadequately supported him and the government of Carthage abandoned him, whether out of lack of supplies or jealousy. Factions of the Carthaginian oligarchy that favored peace soon shouted down the war party.

His army was forced out of Sicily, and Rome regained control. At the battle of Herdonia and Locri Epizephyri, Hannibal asked his brother to bring reinforcements from Iberia. But he was unable to repeat his march across the Alps and was later killed in battle. Mago Barca's head was eventually delivered to his distraught brother. Finally, in 203 B.C., after 15 years of warfare on the Italian peninsula, the general reluctantly returned to Carthage to stave off an invasion by Cornelius Scipio Africanus.

Hannibal entered tenuous negotiations with the Scipio after protracted negotiations. Carthage would lose its European holdings and pay a war indemnity. Rome was not confident that Carthage would honor any treaty terms, but it gained desired concessions from a defeated enemy. The tenuous peace appeared threatened when Carthage had a new surge of confidence due to the return of its leader and a Roman naval defeat at the Gulf of Tunis. But the change in fortunes was short-lived. Scipio defeat Hannibal's cavalry at the battle of Zima and neutralized the effect of his elephants. The Roman general used the Carthaginian's signature move against him and attacked Hannibal's rear flank, causing his formation to collapse. He was defeated and the army surrendered. With the loss of 20,000 troops, Carthage realized that the second Punic War was no longer winnable. The dream of a Carthaginian empire had ended.

Despite being stripped of his command by Carthage's political leadership, Hannibal was able to find a new way to serve his state as a suffette, or chief magistrate. This was not considered a prestigious appointment, but he was able to wield enough power to improve Carthage's financial and judicial systems. The 43-year-old instituted reforms such as restructuring the city-state's economic system and overhauling the 104, a term for Carthage's council of judges.

The city-state entered a period of prosperity.

Proving no good deed goes unpunished, these reforms were Hannibal's final undoing. The economic restructuring made the landed aristocracy fear losing its power. Always jealous of Hannibal, they informed the Roman Senate that Hannibal's new alliance with the Seleucid Empire was part of a plan to invade Italy. Whether it was true or not, Rome demanded Carthage's surrender. Instead, Hannibal went into exile in the court of King Antiochus of Syria in 195 B.C.

Seleucid decided to invade Greece as the first stage of an invasion of Rome. Hannibal offered to lead the army, but he was only placed in command of a small fleet of ships due to the advice of Antiochus' advisors. He then attempted to convince the Seleucid king to invade Italy with an army under his command. The idea was never brought to fruition. Rome, sensing another attack on Italy, went on the offense against the Seleucids, routing them at Thermopylae in 191 BC. They were decisively defeated at Magnesia ad Sipylum in 190 B.C. by Scipio Asiaticus.

To avoid the Romans, Hannibal had to flee once more. He sought refuge in the Armenian court of Artaxias, then Crete, and finally the court of King Prusias I of Bithynia. He served Pursias in an attempt to rally him against Pergamon, Rome's ally. Hannibal served as his naval commander and won victory over King Eumenes II of Pergamon. In one of the naval victories he had large pots filled with venomous snakes thrown onto their ships. He defeated Eumenes in two other battles on land, but then Rome intervened. They threatened Bithynia to give up Hannibal. Rather than surrendering, he poisoned himself in 182 B.C.

Despite failing in his ultimate military objectives, Hannibal's enduring legacy is as one of the greatest strategists of all time. His victory at Cannae and ability to attack the enemy's weakest flank has been replicated by generals as recently as Operation Desert Storm in 1991. U.S. General Norman Schwarzkopf employed this strategy to great success, despite his technological advantages of satellites and F-14s over Hannibal's cavalry, spears, and elephants. He arranged American forces to surround the

Iraqis in a 100-hour war by successfully assaulting their rear flank.

Despite Hannibal's success in battle, it is clear that winning the battle is not equal to winning the war. His inability to build a permanent alliance with Roman cities doomed his invasion.

But perhaps his greatest legacy is inspiring hope amongst those who face impossibly long odds. When told by his generals that crossing the Alps with elephants was impossible, he responded with the Latin phrase *Aut viam inveniam aut faciam* ("I will either find a way, or make one"). Historian Theodore Ayrault Dodge credits this attribute as the chief source of his success and most distinguished part of his legacy.

He praises him as the finest military commander, inspirational figure, and, above all, patriot:

"Hannibal excelled as a tactician. No battle in history is a finer sample of tactics than Cannae. But he was yet greater in logistics and strategy. No captain ever marched to and fro among so many armies of troops superior to his own numbers and material as fearlessly and skillfully as he. No man ever held his own so long or so ably against such odds. Constantly overmatched by better soldiers, led by generals always respectable, often of great ability, he yet defied all their efforts to drive him from Italy, for half a generation. ... As a soldier, in the countenance he presented to the stoutest of foes and in the constancy he exhibited under the bitterest adversity, Hannibal stands alone and unequaled. As a man, no character in history exhibits a purer life or nobler patriotism."

Chapter 3

Julius Caesar (100-44 B.C): History's Greatest Statesman and the Primogenitor of Imperial Power

Brutus and Cassius – the assassins of Julius Caesar – learned the hard way that Hell hath no fury like an emperor scorned. In Dante's *Inferno,* the two Roman senators are condemned to spend all eternity in the lowest circle of Hell. There, they are perpetually chewed in two of Satan's three mouths, along with Judas Iscariot, continuously being rended but never killed. The unfortunate souls make a triumvirate of the most treacherous men in history and constitute the worst of all sinners – traitors to their benefactors.

The Italian poet Dante's reference to the Romans was not for mere literary effect. He and his countrymen still mourned the betrayal and murder of Julius Caesar 1,300 years earlier. Had he not died, they supposed, Italy would have never fractured into small city-states as it was in the Middle Ages. It perhaps could still have held the seat of global power.

Julius Caesar sat on such a throne in his lifetime and earned his auspicious reputation by losing almost no battle. He personified the height of military and political power. His surname "Caesar" – which was common in his lifetime and had no special meaning – became posthumously synonymous with "king," "emperor" in multiple languages ("Kaiser" in German, "Czar" in Russian, "Qaysar" in Arabic, and "Sezer" in Turkish). His conquests changed not only the Roman Empire but also the political and military history of Western Civilization.

Yet despite his success, he was not a career military man. His career began late and was as much a product of his ambition as his allegiance to Rome. Nonetheless, his ruthless approach and his strategic superiority were continuously proven. He extended the Roman Empire's domains as far north as Britain and as far south as Egypt. Unlike Hannibal, his political acumen matched his military ability. Caesar successfully transmuted his battlefield victories into political expansion and permanent government that lasted for centuries after his death.

Julius Caesar was born into a patrician, if not prominent, Roman family. It claimed lineage to the Trojan Aeneas, which according to legend was the son of Venus. Caesar's father governed the province of Asia. Little else is recorded of his early childhood, but it is known that at 16, his father died and he became the head of the household. Caesar gained a powerful sponsor when his aunt married Gaius Marius, a high-ranking official in the Roman Republic.

A civil war broke out between Marius and his rival, Lucius Cornelius Sulla. As Marius' position grew, he appointed Caesar the chief priest of Jupiter. It was a religious position that came with significant political power, as was the case in the theocratically colored military oligarchy that constituted Rome's government. He married Cornelia, the daughter of Marius' ally, Lucius Cornelius Cinna. Caesar's appointment was short-lived; when Sulla gained the upper hand over Marius, he lost his appointment and his dowry. Despite his rapid decline in fortunes, the young priest refused to give up his wife. His mother was able to intervene through her family and save him from execution by helping him flee from Rome.

Caesar joined the army as the simplest means of escape. The beginning of his military career was respectable but unremarkable. He returned to Rome after Sulla had died and took up a legal career. Caesar quickly gained a reputation as a talented prosecutor, using his tremendous oratory ability to bring corrupt government officials to justice. The position required travel, which presented danger on his trips to the fringes of the Republic.

In one such episode Caesar was kidnapped by pirates as he crossed the Aegean Sea. His powerful personality did not abate despite the threat to his person. When his captors demanded a ransom of 20 talents of silver, he demanded that it be raised to 50 in keeping with his social stature. In perhaps one of the most memorable story of revenge in history, he also promised the pirates that upon his release he would crucify them personally. They thought he was jesting. When the ransom was paid, he raised a fleet, pursued and captured the pirates, and imprisoned them. All of them were crucified on his authority.

His political career once again turned to military affairs when in 69 B.C. he became a military tribune and quaestor in Spain. His wife died the same year; two years later he married the daughter of Pompeia, the granddaughter of Sulla. In 63 B.C., on his return from Spain, he entered a Roman election to obtain the position of Pontifex Maximus, or Chief Priest of Rome. In a hotly contested election, he defeated two prominent opponents. After his term finished, he returned to Spain, where he served as governor. Despite his rising fortunes in politics, Caesar's financial situation was still weak. He formed an alliance with Marcus Lucinius Crassus, one of Rome's richest men, who paid off some of his debts and provided surety for others in return for political support.

He returned to the provinces to complete his governorship in order to avoid prosecution for his debts. In Spain, he led Roman troops to victory against local tribes and reformed the legal system. After his term, Caesar returned to Rome to stand for consul, the highest magistracy in the republic. He divorced Pompeia and married Calpurnia, the daughter of another powerful senator. He formed an alliance known as the "First Triumvirate" with Crassus and his political rival, Pompey. It was a cabal that controlled public business through their money and influence. The alliance was complete with the marriage of Pompey to Caesar's daughter, Julia.

Using strong-arm tactics, Caesar collaborated with Pompey to provide land grants as compensation for Pompey's former soldiers in Asia. His term as Spain's governor gave him a five-year immunity from prosecution, which he would need to continue expanding his influence. Though he was in line for another governorship, the aristocracy wanted to limit his power. Their fears may have been correct; nonetheless, Caesar was able to overrule them and became governor of Cisalpine Gaul and Illyricum. When Transalpine Gaul's leader died, he gained an additional governorship.

As discussed in Chapter 1, Caesar experienced an existential crisis when the 30-something statesman looked up on a statue of Alexander the Great and realized that the Macedonian general had accomplished his extraordinary conquests before reaching his age. As a result, he began his Gaul campaign in 58 B.C. as a means of self-validation that he may join the pantheon of greatest generals in history. His other purposes for the campaign were for personal glory and to end his debts.

The campaign was no easy task, as the area was unstable due to the Germanic tribes' fierce tenacity in guerrilla warfare. Caesar's first battle came against the Helvetii in the Battle of Bibracte. The Helvetii attempted to cross into Transalpine Gaul. When they were stopped, they traveled through the lands of the Aedui, a Roman ally. When the Helvetii were ordered to turn over hostages, they refused and continued onward. At Bibracte, the Helvetii thought Romans had retreated in order to resupply. In fact, the Romans occupied the high ground and rained javelins down on the Helvetiis from above, followed by an infantry attack. The Helvetii had no choice but to retreat after their supplies were captured.

In the same year, the Suebi tribe threatened to cross the Rhine and overrun the Audeui, violating a treaty with Rome. Caesar met with the Suebi commander Ariovistus to gain assurance of their intentions, but he had little confidence that Ariovistus was an honest broker; the chieftain had already crossed the Rhine, and his troops had initiated skirmishes against the Romans. Caesar prepared for attack. He lined up his army into a three-column formation. As the Germans launched their assault, Roman cavalry commander Publius Crassus led a counterstrike. The German line retreated quickly. Over 100,000 Suebi were killed. They never crossed the Rhine again.

In 57 B.C., Caesar's next challenge was against the Galia Belgica, located in modern-day Belgium and northern France. The Belgae were considered to be fierce warriors and possess uncommon bravery. The tribes allied unanimously against the Roman army, raising up forces that numbered up 288,000. Caesar avoided meeting the massive force directly in battle and preferred small cavalry skirmishes with contingents of tribesmen. His strategy was to isolate the tribes and break them down in piecemeal fashion.

Caesar's initial attacks involved the infantry, cavalry, light troops, and archers. He followed up with an attack using siege towers. As the tribes fell to the Roman army one by one, the area soon came under conquest. The last holdouts among the Belgae were the Nervii. They knew that the Roman campaign could be stopped if their supply lines were separated from the cavalry. The Nervii first attacked the cavalry followed by the laborers setting up the encampment. Caesar realized that quick action was necessary. He hastily assembled a counterattacking force. He himself led a charge, encouraging his men to push forward in the battle. The Romans made steady progress, but the Nervii continued to hold strong on the right flank. The valiant Nervii realized that the end of the battle was approaching when they caught site of two Roman legions delayed behind the baggage train. These fresh troops were able to join with the existing troops and finally defeat them.

Contending with fierce tribesmen was the most salient feature of the Gaul campaign. In 56 B.C., Roman messengers went to the Gallic tribes to demand grain and provisions for the troops. The messengers were seized by the Veneti, a coastal maritime people living in modern-day Brittany. They promised the messengers' release only upon the release of their own hostages. Caesar was in little mood to negotiate or have his soldiers used as bargaining chips. He stormed their strongholds by engineering moles and raising siege works in order to enter their defenses. The Veneti fled in their trading vessels, which were sail-driven and lacked oars. Junius Brutus took charge of the Roman naval fleet and destroyed the Veneti sails and rigging. When the winds suddenly died down, the Veneti were left stranded. They surrendered. Caesar made an example out of their treachery against the republic to other Gallic tribes. Everyone on the governing council was beheaded; the rest were sold into slavery.

In 55 B.C., Caesar made the first of two trips across the English Channel to Britain. The trip was unsuccessful due to a storm and nearly ended in disaster. In his second trip he defeated the Catuvellauni tribe, but failed to penetrate far into the islands, leave a garrison, or take steps toward absorbing it into Roman rule. The island remained independent for over a century afterwards.

His reputation as a competent battle commander did not go unnoticed by the Imperial Senate. In addition to crafting his own military victories, Caesar was frequently called to difficult battles to assist Roman generals who were unsuccessful at quelling rebellions. The Gauls revolted in 54 BC, led by the Eburones under Ambirix. They won a major victory at Atuatuca Tngrorum in what is now Belgium. Caesar arrived at the battle scene to stave off further Roman losses. He, in turn, destroyed the Eubrones. A second uprising by Vencingetorix, chief of Arvemi, attempted to cut off the Roman army from its supply lines, prompting Caesar to return from Italy and lead the attack. He captured the town of Avaricum but failed to do so at Georgiva. Caesar then besieged Vencingetorix at Alesia and crushed its supplies lines. With this decisive victory, the Gallic Wars had finally come to an end. Caesar had established himself as Rome's most effective and powerful military commander.

The end of the war also meant the end of the First Triumvirate. Crassus had died in battle, and Pompey, the leader of the Senate, had aligned himself with Caesar's opponents. Pompey ordered Caesar to return to Rome in 50 B.C. due to his term as governor finishing. Caesar was concerned that he would be prosecuted if he lacked magisterial immunity. In the most famous move of his career, which spawned a universal cliché of committing an indelible action, he crossed the Rubicon River with a single legion. As he stood on the banks of the river, he quoted the Athenian Meander with the Greek phrase "The die is cast."

This signaled the beginning of civil war. Pompey and the Senate escaped south as Caesar was declared dictator, despite their having more troops.

Caesar first went to Spain to defeat Pompey's lieutenants, leaving Rome in charge of Mark Antony. He defeated them following a 27-day route-march. Caesar then pursued Pompey to Greece and defeated him at Pharsalus. Pompey escaped and Caesar pursued him to Egypt. He finally caught up him, but not in the manner that the new emperor expected; Caesar was presented with his former ally's head shortly after Pompey's death by assassination from counselors to king Ptolemy XIII. Caesar wept at the insulting death to the great military and political leader. He had Pompey's assassins executed.

While in Egypt, he involved himself in the civil war in order extend his political influence over the state. He aligned with Cleopatra VII, sister of King Ptolemy XIII. In 47 B.C., Caesar was besieged in Alexandria with a small force of 4,000. The child pharaoh Ptolemy fled from Alexander and hoped to cut off his supply chains. Caesar convinced his ally Mithridates of Pergamum to join him in Egypt. Together their combined forces of 20,000 met Ptolemy in the Battle of the Nile. His army used pikes, while the Roman forces attacked with spears, shields, and swords. Caesar attacked the Egyptians under a shower of spears and overwhelmed them by getting past the Egyptian pike's point with their shields and laying them about with their short swords. Rome won a decisive victory. Caesar now ruled Egypt and put Cleopatra and her brother Ptolemy XIV on the throne. He lingered on in Egypt for several more months and had liaisons with the youthful queen. Although they were unable to marry under Roman law due to her not being a citizen, the two reportedly had a child, Caeserion.

Caesar's final two military victories were against Pontus in the Middle East, Pompey's sons in Spain, and his remaining senatorial supporters in Africa. Both victories were executed swiftly and took mere months. This victory earned him a decade-long appointment as dictator. He used this enormous political capital in his final years to tie up military loose ends left dangling on the periphery of the empire and executing political reform. Caesar centralized the government in order to curb armed resistance in the provinces, reduce corruption, and homogenize the empire, from Rome out to the peripheries. New legislation encompassed everything from debt reform and term limits for governors to grain purchase. He replaced the Roman lunar calendar with a solar calendar, known as the Julian calendar. A police force was established. Carthage and Corinth were rebuilt. The Senate named him censor for life and Father of the Fatherland.

He did not shy away from his subjects' tendency to engage in emperor worship. Minted coins bore his image, and statues were erected in the Senate of him sitting upon a golden chair. When he returned to Rome after his final military victories, triumphal games were held that involved gladiator contests, a naval battle on the flooded basin at the Field of Mars, beast-hunts involving 400 lions, and thousands of captives fighting to the death at the Circus Maximus.

But he was not universally beloved. Certain aristocratic members disdained his new status as dictator for life and the destruction of the republic. Factions formed against him. On the 15th of March in 44 B.C. he awoke not feeling well. A fortune teller told him to beware the Ides of March. Furthermore, his wife dreamed of him being murdered and pleaded with him not to leave the house.

Ignoring her pleas, he listened to his close confidant Brutus to attend a Senate meeting. A group of senators had called him to the forum to read a petition that asked him to return power to the Senate. When he reached the meeting hall, he found himself surrounded by a group of senators. Per the legend of his death, Tillius Cimber knelt down before him and then grabbed his purple robe. According to Suetonius, he cried to Cimber, "Why, this is violence!" Casca then produced his dagger and made a glancing thrust at the dictator's neck. Caesar caught his arm and said "Casca, you villain, what are you doing?"

The other members of the conspiracy assisted him and

began striking Caesar. They plunged their daggers into him, including Brutus. Upon laying eyes upon his friend, he gasped with his last breath, *Et tu Brute?* The commander who had spread imperial rule from Gaul to Egypt died at the base of a status of Pompey inflicted by 23 knife wounds, bleeding out on the marble floor.

Caesar's life came to an end, but the empire he created existed for four more centuries in its unified form, and 14 centuries in the form of its daughter state as the Byzantine Empire. His legacy as a victorious commander is well-earned, but his true esteem by military historians does not come from his success in battle. History is littered with courageous commanders such as Genghis Khan, Alexander, and Tamerlane whose empires crumbled shortly after their deaths. What distinguished Caesar was making those conquests sustainable through his shrewd maneuvering and political acumen. This was not an easy matter, as demonstrated by the shaky alliance of the First Triumvirate. But it is a legacy that not even the most able of commanders attained.

He was recognized as Rome's greatest statesman, even in forthcoming decades. The Roman biographer Plutarch claims that, "If one [were to] compare him with such men as Fabius and Scipio and Metellus, and with the men of his own time or a little before him, like Sulla, Marius, the two Luculli, or even Pompey himself, whose fame for every sort of military excellence was at this time flowering out and reaching to the skies, Caesar will be found to surpass them all in his achievements."

Perhaps his strongest recommendation comes from no less than Jesus Christ himself. In the early first century Jewish religious leaders laid a logical trap at the teacher's feet, wanting to end his ministry for fear of him stirring up an Israeli rebellion against Rome and bringing down the imperial sword upon their necks. They asked him if it was incumbent to pay taxes to the Roman Empire, a pagan political entity many Israelites believed would be defeated by the coming Messiah. He held up a denarius to the crowd that bore the visage of Caesar and enquired as to whose picture was engraved upon it. Receiving his answer, he said, "Rend unto Caesar what is Caesar's and unto God what is God's."

Such is the legacy of a man who was so powerful that even the founder of Christianity acknowledged that he controlled the political domains of the Earth.

Chapter 4:

Khalid ibn al-Walid (592-642): The Sword of God' and Commander-in-Chief of the Muslim Caliphate

Khalid ibn al-Walid – dubbed "The Sword of God" by Muhammad – had a strange relationship with the Islamic religion. On the one hand he was directly responsible for its explosion out of the Arabian Peninsula in the early seventh century. He led its armies in the conquest of Iraq, Jordan, Palestine, and Syria, often times against superior forces. Khalid never lost a battle in his decades-long career, even destroying the Persian Empire and crippling the Byzantine Empire.

His tactical successes at the Battle of Yarmouk and Walaja by the use of mounted warriors proved him to be one of the greatest cavalry commanders in history. He was commended by Prince Ukaid of Domat ul Jandal, who at the time was advising an enemy of Khalid, that, "No man is his equal in war. No people face Khalid in battle, be they strong or weak, but are defeated. Take my advice and make peace with him."

Yet his successes also made him a paradoxical figure in the religion's infancy. The commander was the only general ever to lead a force that defeated Mohammed's army in combat. This defeat threatened to undercut Islam at its birth, since Mohammed often substantiated his claims to prophecy by his military success as proof of Allah's blessing. This paradox was only resolved by Khalid's conversion to Islam following a truce after the Battle of Uhud.

However, his dazzling victories under the reigns of Caliphs abu Bakar and 'Umar made both men fear that he would undercut them and possibly gain enough popular support to wage a rebellion. 'Umar resolved his fears by stripping the general of command and discharging him from the military. Khalid spent his "retirement" and the rest of his career as a foot soldier, smashing swords through his opponents in pitched battle.

His command record includes victories in over 100 battles and zero defeats. His conquests spread a new religion beyond its Arabian beginnings and into Persian and Byzantium, biting off enormous chunks of land from the world's two most powerful empires. Equally as important, Khalid ibn al-Walid was a brilliant strategist who was never hesitant to battle a larger force. Without his leadership, the armies of Islam may have been destroyed and the religion would have been consigned to the dustbin of history as a failed heterodox movement. His conquests changed the history of the Middle East and the fortunes of Islam, propelling it to its current position today.

Khalid was born in Mecca to a wealthy family in 584. He belonged to the Quraish, the tribe from which Muhammad originated. His father, Walid ibn al-Mughirah, was a respected and generous leader who opposed the nascent Islamic religion. Muhammad had suffered a falling out with the tribe following the death of his uncle, Abu Talib, the leader of his clan, in 619. Mecca's elites also opposed his prophetic career, particularly after he fled to Medina. Khalid's father was a devoted caretaker of the Kaaba, a sacred site in the pre-Islamic period. Walid provided Khalid with a military upbringing because he was the chief of the Banu Makhzum, a clan of the Quraish tribe that was responsible for matters of warfare. Khaid was a strong young man and his training as a youth prepared him for a life as a soldier and warrior. According to legend, he even took bits of poison to build up his immunity.

He was described by chroniclers as being tall, strong, and with broad shoulders. He exhibited enormous physical strength and was a champion wrestler. Khalid was, like many nomads in his tribe, was an effective horseman and proficient in weaponry. He was deadly with the spear, lance, bow, and, of course, the sword. Moreover, he did not handle defeat or failure with grace. As a young man, he had endured a Quraish defeat by Mohammed's army and vowed vengeance.

Khalid received his chance at the battle of Uhud. The pretext for battle was the continual warfare between the upstart Islamic religion and the tribes of Arabia. The Quraish confederacy fought many battles with the Muslim community at Medina, as Mohammed and his followers had raided many merchant caravans. The Muslim army was ready for battle, but the Quraish had superiority in numbers. In 625 they faced each other at Mount Uhud in northwestern Arabia. The Quraish were able to break the Muslim army ranks, but they regrouped and counterattacked with their skilled archers. The Quraish persisted but were eventually cornered by the Muslims.

The Quraish remembered their previous defeat at Badr in 624 to the Muslim army and ordered a retreat, leaving their equipment behind. The Muslims saw the Quraish leaving the battlefield and focused on their plunder sitting openly at the unprotected camp. In a breach of Muhammad's orders, the Muslim archers abandoned their posts to join in the plundering. Khalid saw this opportunity and assembled his cavalry force. He counterattacked the preoccupied Muslim army, bringing chaos to their ranks. As he attacked, the other Quraish tribesmen followed suit and defeated their Medinan adversaries, even injuring Muhammad. In 627 he fought the same army in the battle of Trench, his final battle against Muhammad's forces before converting to Islam.

After the battle of Trench, a 10-year peace agreement was agreed upon between the Muslims and Quraish of Mecca in 628. With peace concluded, Khalid began to explore the tenants of the Islamic religion. His brother, Walid bin Walid, had been captured in the battle of Uhud and, despite being ransomed, returned to Muhammad's cause and converted to Islam. Walid in turn wrote letters to Khalid in an attempt to convert him.]

Parts of the religion appealed to him, particularly its emphasis on monotheism. Even before his conversion he rejected the idolatry that was widely practiced in Arabia. Muhammad was confident that a man of such martial abilities and steely temperament would eventually come around. According to a chronicler, he told Walid "A man like Khalid can't keep himself from Islam for long." The prophet was correct. In 629, he joined Muhammad in Medina and declared his fealty both as a soldier and as a religious disciple.

In 629, Muhammad sent an invitation to the Ghaassanid ruler of Syrian, a Byzantine vassal, to convert to Islam. While his envoy was en route to the royal court to deliver this message, a Ghaasanid chieftain killed him, setting off a diplomatic incident. Muhammad sent out a force to avenge the attack, led by Zayd ibn Harithat.

In the battle of Mu'tah, Zayd and his two commanders were killed, wiping out the chain of command and leaving the troops hopelessly outnumbered. Khalid was given a battlefield promotion to lead 3,000 men against a force of 200,000 Byzantine and Ghaasanid troops. He led a strategic retreat, fooling the enemy into believing that there was a much larger force waiting to attack.

In further acts of psychological warfare, he sent columns behind the main army and joined the Muslim army in small bands to create the illusion of battle reinforcements arriving. During this battle, he is said to have broken nine swords in the heat of pitched battle. The Byzantines believed in the fictitious arrival of reinforcements and eventually withdrew. The Muslim forces then safely retreated to Medina. Muhammad, realizing Khalid's tactical brilliance, conferred upon him the title "The sword of Allah."

A year later, Khalid commanded one of the four bands that entered and conquered Mecca from four different routes. The entry was peaceful, although Khalid did face resistance. He was also involved in the conquest of Tubak and two expeditions to Dawmut ul-Jandal in Arabia; one to convert the Prince Ukaydir, and a second to destroy the pagan idol Wad. He was then sent to convert the Banu Jadhimah tribe. When they resisted, he began to execute its members. This angered Muhammad, who believed the violence to be unmerited despite ordering it in similar circumstances and made restitution by offering compensation to the victims. In 631, he participated in the ailing Muhammad's farewell pilgrimage. The prophet of Islam died that same year.

After Muhammad's death, rebellion threatened to erupt among the tribes of the infant religion, and Khalid was caught in the middle of the imbroglio. He ultimately came to a place of power within the winning faction. The Muslim community chose a replacement as the leader of their religion. This person was known as the Caliph ("successor" or "representative" in Arabic) and the domain of his leadership was known as the Caliphate.

Like the pope of the Middle Ages, the Caliph maintained both spiritual and political power over his subjects. But unlike the pope, the Caliph was recognized as the universal head of his religion for only a few decades before the community split. The first Caliph was Abu Bakr (632-634). He was among the first converts to Islam, and the father-in-law to Muhammad, who married his daughter A'ishah. The second was 'Umar (634-644), who fought the Byzantine Empire to the north and completely enveloped the Persian Empire in 636, which had existed for over 1,000 years. And at the forefront of these armies was Khalid.

Caliph Abu Bakr quickly quelled these revolts, launched by rebels who stated that they had submitted to Muhammad as a prophet but not to his successor. He sent out Khalid and his armies against these powerful tribes in central Arabia in a series of battles known as the Riddah wars. In securing peace, he went to Nejd, where the Banu Tamim lived. Most of the tribes within this region pledged allegiance to Abu Bakr.

However, local power broker Sheik Mlik ibn Nuwayrh was reluctant to make a similar pledge. He agreed to pay tribute but aligned with Sajjah, who claimed she was a prophetess. When confronted with these crimes, Sheik Mlik ibn Nuwayrh openly disrespected Abu Bakr with flippant attitudes toward his orders that Khalid conveyed to him: "Your master said this, your master said that," he scoffed. Khalid ordered the execution of the sheik, carried it out, and married the sheik's widow, Layla. Abu Bakr found the killing of a fellow Muslim and the marriage to be abhorrent. He threatened to have Khalid stoned. This ultimately did not come to pass. By 632, all rebellions had been crushed.

Arabia was now united under Abu Bakr's central authority. The elderly caliph now turned his gaze outward toward his powerful neighbors. In 633, he put Khalid in charge of the caliphate's campaign in the lower Mesopotamia area of the Persian Empire, despite his earlier rebuke of the young general. He led a force of 18,000 soldiers to capture the empire's richest provinces. Khalid met little resistance among the Iraqis, who quickly realized that they would fare better as Muslim subjects than as Persian subjects, and greeted them as liberators.

His successes against the Persians quickly piled up. He quickly won the Battle of Chains in April 633, the first battle between the Rashidun Caliphate and the Persian Empire, and the Battle of the River mere weeks later. In this second battle, many Persian veterans and survivors of the Battle of Chains abandoned their army and joined the Muslims, fighting against their former comrades mere days after the fact.

Khalid's most famous victory came at the Battle of Walajaa in May 633. Khalida and al-Muthanna ibn Haritha faced a Persian army reinforced by Arab allies that totaled numbers at least three times the size of their own army. He implemented a variation of Hannibal's famous double envelopment maneuver by surrounding the enemy as it advanced and then crushed it with two flanks. This was only the second time in history that this extremely difficult maneuver was successfully executed. Military historians believe that Khalid developed his own maneuver independent of Hannibal, as he was likely not familiar with Roman military history.

He faced the Persians with 5,000 cavalry forces and 10,000 foot soldiers. The Persian commander Andarzaghar trusted in his numerical superiority and allowed the Muslim army to charge first, hoping to wear them out and launch a vicious counterattack. The Persian strategy worked in the beginning of the battle, as Andarzaghar was able to replace men in the front lines with reinforcements, holding back Khalid's forces.

The Persians then counterattacked with their heavy cavalry against the Muslim front. Khalid allowed the center of his formation to fall back as the two flanks held their ground. At his order, the light cavalry charged, attacked, retreated, regrouped, and attacked again. Their crescent formation wore down the Persians rapidly and their heavy cavalry was too slow to respond. The Muslim army attacked their flanks, encircling them. The Persians were completely surrounded. Their numbers were cut down to all but a few thousand that escaped.

That Khalid was able to successfully execute the maneuver so early in his career proved his acumen as a strategist. After Walaja he won the Battle of Ullais in mid-May of 633. Later that month, Al-Hira, the regional Persian capital of lower Mesopotamia, fell. The inhabitants agreed to pay tribute following negotiators with their conquerors. He then laid siege to Anbar, which was not nearly as easy to conquer due to heavy resistance from the inhabitants. In the end Khalid broke the siege by using Muslim archers to force surrender.

He had conquered much of the northern Euphrates region. But conquest did not mean a consolidation of power. Khalid had to answer a call for relief from northern Iraq in which the Muslim General Ayaz bin Ghanam was trapped by rebels in his army. He went to his rescue and defeated the rebels at Daumat-ul-jandal. While he was distracted with putting down the mutiny, Persian forces prepared to counter the rising Muslim threat. The forces included Persians and Christian Arab auxiliaries, based in four camps at Hanafiz, Zumiel, Sanni, and Muzieh. Khalid, once again leading numerically inferior forces, sought to attack each camp at once rather than face a unified force. He split his army into three separate units and attacked each Persian army. The strategy worked. After defeating a combined Persian, Byzantine, and Arab Christian force at Firaz, Khalid had conquered Iraq.

Khalid was next ordered to conquer Byzantine Syria. This

was indeed a tall order. The historical area in question is much larger than present-day Syria and its domains included the modern nations Jordan, Israel, Palestine, Lebanon, and Southern Turkey. His army was composed of 23,000 soldiers led by four generals. The army marched city-by-city in small battles. Khalid then began a three-day march through the mountains towards Damascus. He stopped before reaching it in order to assist Abu Ubaidah ibn al-Jarrah, the chief commander along the Syrian-Arab border, who requested emergency reinforcement.

Entering Syria directly from Iraq required passing through the Syrian Desert. The army did not have enough time to stock up on adequate provisions for the march. As a result, tradition says that soldiers walked two days through the Syrian Desert without any water. They finally reached an oasis but had no means to carry water with them. Khalid, well-acquainted with Bedouin culture, used a method of known among desert-traversing traders to carry water into the most desiccated parts of the desert.

The pack animals of the army were exclusively camels, which could drink dozens of gallons of water in minutes and were capable of storing 50 gallons at one time. They were also capable of storing fresh water in their stomachs, making them walking water storage devices. The armies resumed their marched through the desert, and then slaughtered them as their thirst required and drank from the contents of their stomachs.

The army arrived in Syria in June 634 and immediately captured border towns. Khalid then preceded to Basra, where he assisted Shari eel bin Hassana's 4,000 troops against 12,000 Byzantines. When Khalid's 9,000 soldier army arrived, the Byzantines retreated to the city's castle. After a siege, they returned to the battlefield and were defeated. Over 90,000 Byzantine troops gathered at Ajnadayn, where they were defeated by 20,000 Muslim forces. This was the tipping point that signaled the end of Byzantine power in Syria and the coming dominance of Islam.

Before the battle began, a Christian bishop attempted to

negotiate a peaceful resolution. Khalid in response offered the traditional Islamic terms prior to battle or city siege: surrender, conversion to Islam, or agreement to pay the *jizya*, an Islamic poll-tax administered to non-Muslims. The bishop refused. As both forces assembled into battle formation, Khalid told his forces, including his archers, to show restraint.

The battle commenced with skirmishes between individual troops, an advantage for the Muslim army. A soldier named Dharar Ibn al Azwar, also known as the "half-naked warrior" – due to fighting without a shirt or shield – moved forward using in equipment taken from a dead soldier. As he removed the equipment and the Byzantines recognized him, several officers challenged him to combat. During this dueling, Khalid ordered more elite warriors to join the battle and eventually launched a full-scale attack. The first day ended in a stalemate with no clear victor but heavy casualties resulted on both sides.

The second day started by Byzantine commander Theodorus challenging Khalid to a duel. As it began, Theodorus grabbed Khalid and called for the Byzantine troops to assist. The troops arrived and leader stripped to the waist and revealed himself to actually be Dharar Ibn al Azwar. In his shock, Theodorus was killed. The battle began once again, and Khalid unleashed his reserve troops.

The Byzantines finally retreated with the Muslim cavalry in pursuit, which killed more soldiers than the battle itself. The final tally of casualties was 450 Muslims and 70,000 Romans. Although it was a Muslim route, they did lose many senior commanders. The Roman Emperor Heraclius realized that the local forces were not enough to repel the Muslims and that he needed to deploy the elite Imperial Army.

Khalid continued his campaign of Byzantine conquest and returned to Damascus. He defeated the Emperor Heraclius's son-in-law, Thomas, at the Battle of Yakosa and won the Battle of Maraj-al-Safar. On the August 20, 634, he reached Damascus, where he defeated the Byzantines at Sanita-al-Uqab. After three Byzantine attacks, Khalid's army attacked Damascus and gave them three days to convert, submit to the *jizya* or abandon the city with their families. The Byzantines abandoned the city, but the Muslim cavalry caught up with them and attacked. The Muslim army, however, received a temporary setback when Calipha Abu Bakr died during the siege. Khalid's cousin 'Umar was immediately appointed as his replacement in 634.

Perhaps due to jealousy for the military commander's fantastic success, or mere family rivalry, 'Umar replaced Khalid with another commander as the leader of the Muslim forces in 634. There was ostensible animosity between the two, so in order to avert any suspicions of pettiness, Umar declared that his dismissal of the popular general was to prove that Khalid's success was the work of Allah, not his strategic genius. He may have done so to prevent a cult of personality from growing around Khalid before it began. The former commander's response to his dismissal was one of allegiance: "If Abu Bakr is dead and 'Umar is Caliph, then we hear and obey." 'Umar appointed Abu Ubaidah ib al Jarrah as the new leader of the Muslim army. He in turn appointed Khalid as an advisor and cavalry commander.

Khalid was true to his word. Abu Ubaidah sent him to salvage a dire situation near Zahle, close to modern-day Beirut. Abu Ubaidah had sent a small detachment to an annual fair held at Abu-al-Quds to issue a surprise attack. The Muslim commander had miscalculated the size of their enemy forces. There a large Byzantine and Christian Arab garrison guarded the fair and it quickly surrounded the small Muslim force. When Khalid arrived to assist the commander, he engaged them in the Battle of Abu-al-Quds. He not only defeated the Byzantines, but carried off significant plunder from the fair, along with hundreds of captured prisoners.

Central Syria was now captured, and Palestine was cut off from direct communication with the Byzantine capital of Constantinople. Syria had fragmented, and it was now a matter of time before for the Muslim armies completely enveloped the Byzantine Empire's most prosperous province. The next goal was to destroy the garrison at Fahl, an important supply center and key to the defense of Arabia and Palestine. The Byzantines flooded the plain, located 500 feet below sea level, by blocking the Jordan River in order to divert the army. The Muslim army was delayed but ultimately defeated them at the Battle of Fahl in January 635.

Growing desperate, Emperor Heraclius decided to take advantage of the Muslim force's smaller size at Damascus since half the army had moved south to capture Palestine. Heraclius sent General Theodras to recapture the city, along with half his army toward Damascus to launch a surprise attack on the Muslim army. Khalid, however, had an excellent spy network and the surprise attack failed. He attacked General Theodras with his Mobile guard and routed him at the second battle of Damascus.

Abu Ubaida then sent him to capture Emesa. It surrendered, as did Hamma City. Khalid continued to conquer cities; however, Emesa and Qinasareen broke their treaties, and Abu Ubaida dispatched Khalid once again in order to attack the city. After three battles and two sieges, the city was finally captured in March of 636.

In late spring of 636, Khalid received word from captured Byzantine prisoners that Emperor Heraclius was assembling a major campaign to take back Syria with as many as 2,000,000 troops. The emperor had consistently underestimated Khalid and the Muslim armies, hoping to avoid large pitched battles by isolated small Muslim forces. A full-scale, head on battle was now decided as the only plausible course of military action.

The Muslim leaders gathered to plan a counter strategy. Abu Ubaida took Khalid's advice to combine forces and meet at Yarmouk, as it allowed for open battle and the mobile Muslim light cavalry to engage the slower Byzantine heavy cavalry on their terms. The Byzantine army engaged them in mid-July.

The Battle of Yarmouk occurred in mid-August. Khalid was given total command of the army. He was fighting the largest military force in his career. The first four days were spent in a defensive, countering strategy to the Byzantine forces. The battle went back and forth. Although at times each side broke out, there was no clear advantage. On day four, a successful attack by Byzantine archers resulted in injuries and a Muslim retreat, but it did not turn the direction of the battle. On day five, Byzantine commander Vahan wanted to discuss a truce. Khalid decided that this was an indication of Byzantine reluctance and decided to press his advantage.

He ensured that all exit paths for the Byzantine army were guarded. He then drew up a bold plan of attack for day six. It involved his massed cavalry driving the Byzantine cavalry completely off the battlefield, leaving their infantry exposed to the Muslim cavalry at their flanks and rear. Simultaneously, a determined attack from his army would strike the Byzantine's left flank and push them toward the ravine to the west. The final day of the battle arrived on August 20, 636.

Khalid ordered an infantry attack on the Byzantine front while his cavalry attack their left and rear flanks. The Muslim right wing attacked the Byzantine front, which caused their left wing to collapse, resulting in disorder. Vahan attempted to regroup the heavy cavalry to regroup and counterattack, but it was too late to stop the Muslim cavalry. Khalid had wheeled his cavalry back and concentrated on the Byzantine cavalry squadrons.

They fled by the only available escape path, leaving the infantry exposed. Khald turned to the Byzantine's left center, which was holding back his two-pronged attack. His cavalry attacked its rear, breaking it apart. Their columns collapse and a general Byzantine retreat began. Khalid's superior topographical knowledge of the battlefield prepared him for this outcome. He took his cavalry north to block the escape path, forcing the Byzantines to a bridge at Ayn al Dhakar.

It had already been captured by Khalid the night before and was blocked by his soldiers. The Byzantine troops were completely surrounded. Some were pushed into the ravines while others were killed when they attempted to swim away, only to be dashed up against the rocks. Although a few soldiers managed escape, the Muslims took no prisoners. They handed the Christian army an overwhelming and crushing defeat.

The Battle of Yarmouk is considered to be one of the most decisive in history. The Byzantine Empire was doomed in the Levant. Arab armies were positioned in such a way that they could threaten the whole of the empire (and they would do so in later decades, when they laid siege to Constantinople itself). Islam had permanently established itself in Byzantium's most beloved province.

After Yarmouk, the Muslims set to conquer the holy city of Jerusalem in 637. Although they now faced a demoralized and weakened Byzantine army, the city's defensive systems made for a difficult conquest. Many of the Christian survivors of Yarmouk had taken shelter here and lacked provisions. After a four-month siege, the starving refugees and soldiers eventually capitulated and Jerusalem fell. The citizens agreed to surrender, but only to the caliph himself. Amr ibn al-Aas, a corps commander (and an infamous figure in history for allegedly ordering the burning of the Great Library of Alexandria), suggested that Khalid be sent as caliph for the surrender terms since he bore a strong resemblance to his cousin 'Umar.

Following Jerusalem's capture, Khalid fought several more battles in northern Syria, including Hazir and Quasreen, before moving on to Antioch and Aleppo. At the battle of Hazir, the Byzantine army was completely destroyed, causing even 'Umar to begrudgingly amid Khalid's military ability. Abu Ubaidah and Khalid had captured most of northeast Syria. His final act as commander was conquering the city of Marash in southern Anatolia.

His military career ended when 'Umar charged him with religious immorality and abusing state funds. Regarding the first charge, the caliph's spies informed him that Khalid had bathed in a special substance prepared with an alcoholic mixture while in Emesa. This violated the Islamic prohibition on alcohol, although it was an exceptionally literal interpretation of the law that probably left the religious leaders scratching their heads. Second, Khalid gifted a Persian poet 10,000 dirhams from the state treasury when the later recited a poem in praise of the commander after the conquest. 'Umar used this incident as a pretext to charge Khalid with misappropriating state funds. The charges stuck and the enormously popular commander was forcibly retired.

Abu Ubaidah appointed him governor of Quasreen, but he did not live to serve in this capacity. In 642 Khalid died at home in Emesa, where he had lived since his dismissal from military service. He passed away not as a martyr in battle, as he would have wished, but rather in a bed. According to chroniclers, he expressed this regret with the following sentence: "I've fought in so many battles seeking martyrdom that there is no spot in my body left without a scar or a wound made by a spear or sword. And yet here I am, dying on my bed like an old camel. May the eyes of the cowards never rest."

His onlookers looked upon the deceased commander and considered the marks that enveloped his frame. They were mementos from the dozens of battles in which he had fought in and always won. It was as if they had been the only thing holding together his battle-worn frame in his final years.

The legacy of Khalid as a commander is one of the greatest in history. It was not only that he was able to defeat his enemies, but also that he could adapt his strategy to unforeseen circumstances, terrains, and strategies. Furthermore, he showed strength in losing a political battle by accepting a humiliating dismissal with a soldier's obedience. Putting his allegiance to the cause above all other concerns endeared him to the rank-and-file troops.

Khalid inspires military commanders today for his success in battle despite the numerical inferiority of his own forces. And yet his methods, if used today, would likely bring a general before an international war crimes tribunal at The Hague. To Khalid, a battle was not merely the means to the end of a military victory; it was a method of total violence meant to completely annihilate enemy forces. Terror in the hearts of his enemies always made up for any disadvantage. This is another lesson of Khalid's that lesser generals have unfortunately sought to apply throughout the centuries.

Chapter 5

Genghis Khan (1162-1227): Enemy of Empires -- And Atmospheric Carbon?

In 2011 a team of ecologists from the Carnegie Institute made a startling discovery. They determined that a planetary-wide event between the 13th and 14th centuries caused such widespread death and destruction that millions of acres of cultivated land returned to forest, causing global carbon levels to plummet. This event was bigger than the fall of China's Ming Dynasty or even the Black Death. The team said this event was not produced by nature. It was actually the first, and only, case of successful man-made global cooling. And it was not difficult to guess who was responsible: Genghis Khan and his descendants triggered 40 million deaths in this period, making him one of the bloodiest, and ironically, the greenest, dictators in history.

Through his battles and systematic slaughter, he removed 700 million tons of carbon from the atmosphere, equivalent to the amount released from one year of gasoline use today. Massive depopulation in the domains of his conquest, which covered 22 percent of the earth, resulted in the return of forests and their scrubbing of carbon from the atmosphere. While most environmentalists of today would not approve of his methods (except for some neo-Mathusians such as Sir David Attenborough, who in January 2013 lambasted humans as a "plague on the earth"), they cannot deny that his methods achieved what carbon offsets and gas mileage standards have not. How did a tyrant whose influence was felt all the way through the earth's atmosphere rise to power and accomplish such far-reaching results?

Primarily as an effective battle commander, albeit one so fierce that his brutality superseded his reputation as a military genius. Genghis Khan's ruthlessness was set apart in a culture defined by ruthlessness. But chief to his success was effective planning through forging alliances and tactical efficiency. Off the battlefield, he reformed Mongol tribal society, laid the foundations of a simple but effective government, and provided enough flexibility in his state for rapid expansion across Asia. And expand rapidly it did: from Eastern Asia to Europe, from Persia to Russia, the Empire that Genghis Khan created ruled huge portions of the known civilization. He was a conqueror and an innovator whose lessons are still relevant in discussions of nation building.

His military machine was at its core an extension of Mongolic nomadic life. The most fundamental element of the Mongolian army was the horse. A soldier typically had 3 or 4 horses, which allowed him to travel at high speeds for days without wearing out the animal. In the Hungarian invasion of 1241 the Mongolian army covered up to 100 miles a day, an extraordinary distance at a time when suitable roads were all but non-existent.

A soldier's horse was many things to his rider – it was a means of transportation, a war vehicle, a pack animal, and a source of food and water due to the Mongolian appetite for cooked horse meat and *kimis* – fermented horse milk. Mongolian horses were smaller than their European counterparts and slower over short distances. However, Genghis Khan's cavalry were so lightly armored that they could still outrun their foes. Furthermore, the horses were durable over long distances, enabling the army to achieve far-flung victories.

The provisions necessary for a Mongolian army to wage attack were a fraction of that required by more sedentary enemies in China, Iran, the Middle East and Europe. Their slower, more cumbersome opponents were utterly helpless to wage an effective counterattack against their lighting strikes. As a result, his soldiers were highly mobile and required little in the way of sustenance or supply lines to attack an army or put a city to siege. They did not rely on a complex military apparatus, which made flexibility, mobility, and improvisation possible in the most alien and inhospitable of domains.

Mongolians were also excellent horseback-mounted archers, due to practicing this skill nearly as soon as they could walk. Their horses were equipped with stirrups, which allowed archers to turn their upper body and shoot in any direction, even backwards. Their recurve, composite bows allowed for powerful, long arrow fires. Their bows could shoot arrows over 1,600 feet, and they could hit targets from a distance of 750 feet. It was said according to domestic and foreign chroniclers that rank-and-file archers could hit the wings of birds.

The Mongolian cavalry was the primary unit of their war machine. Six out of 10 members of these forces were light cavalry horse archers; the other four were heavy cavalry armed with lances. Light cavalry would typically circle their enemies on the battlefield, fire arrows from a distance, and retreat. They would then either repeat the encirclement and fire more arrows or feign a major retreat and coax their enemies into pursuit. This was a difficult military maneuver to execute, as inexperienced soldiers could turn a feigned retreat into a real retreat if pressed by an aggressive enemy. But failure came infrequently due to their excellent implementation and lack of familiarity to this strategy by Mongolia's enemies. Following this maneuver, the heavy cavalry appeared and led a sortie against their surprised opponents.

Genghis Khan was born as Temujin in 1162 in Deluun Boldog near Burkhan Khladun in northern Mongolia. At his birth he was observed to have a blood clot in his fist, a sign of his destiny as a great leader, according to custom. His father Yesukhei was a leader in the Borjigin tribe and his mother, Hoelun, was of the Olkhunut tribe. Due to his father's polygamy (common in Mongolian tribal society) he had three brothers, a sister, and two half-brothers. When he was still a boy Yesukhei arranged his marriage to a girl from the Ongirrat tribe named Borte. As per the tradition, Temujin, moved in with Borte's family as a servant to her father Dai Setsen when he was 9. He was to have remained a servant until he, and his betrothed were of marrying age. However, as Yesukhei returned from delivering Temujin, he was poisoned by the Tartars, enemies of the Mongols.

In the years following his father's death, it was Temujin's

mother who taught him the importance of forging alliances to endure difficult circumstances and win important battles. His family was ostracized and had to survive for years on their own by hunting and gathering fruit. When he was 16, Temujin returned to take his bride, Borte Ujin. Shortly after they wed, Borte was kidnapped by Merkit tribesmen and given to their chieftain as a wife. This event proved to be the catalyst that launched Temujin's military career. In a short-lived alliance with Ong-Khan, an ally of his father's, and Jamuka, Temujin aligned a group of men to help him defeat the Merkits and retrieve his wife. He was supplied with 20,000 troops, and the recovery allowed Temujin to build a support base. His popularity and reputation as an effective commander began to grow. In light of his new-found power, Jamuka and Ong-Khan declared war against Temujin, a war which he handily won.

Even at that young age, he observed that the nomadic Mongol tribes were victims of a perpetually weak society due to their endless internal warfare. This kept them powerless against the Chinese Empire to the south, the most technologically and administratively advanced on earth. He learned from his mother that small skirmishes among tribesmen were easily won, but not field battle against imperial armies. Or, perhaps better expressed in a Mongolian adage: breaking a single arrow is simple; breaking multiple arrows proves more challenging.

Temujin's strength was in understanding the power of unity. By the age of 20, he used this wisdom to build an army that set out to destroy individual factions and tribes in what was soon to be his massive Mongol Empire. As he conquered, instead of exiling the region's soldiers and killing the survivors, as was commonly practiced, he absorbed each conquered territory into his domain, under his personal rule. This strategy helped him to expand the Mongol Empire quickly and efficiently, making use of all the talents, skills and abilities available in his newly acquired subjects.

He had two primary directives: dominance and unity. Any tribe that refused to unify under his rule had its leader, and sometimes the entire tribe, obliterated. Temujin, now dubbed "Genghis Khan" (Powerful King), set up an information network of advisers, spies, and strategists to gather intelligence on rival factions intending to challenge his rule. He used that information to implement smart, effective military and political strategies to cut down rival power bases.

As he strengthened the Mongolian tribal confederacy, Genghis implemented other reforms to traditional military practice. He promoted officers based on merit rather than family ties. His was a strict meritocracy in which success and loyalty were rewarded. This was a break from Mongol precedent in which family alliances determined prestige and favor, a system that inevitably led to nepotism and did not reward success or punish failure. Due to his policies, tribal or ethnic divisions did not form in his ranks, ending the feudal alliances that engulfed medieval Mongolia. He offered incentives to warriors for their allegiance in the form of plunder. Furthermore, when Genghis captured a tribe, he assimilated the captured and offered them protection.

He reformed the army to a simple, but effective system. Mongol soldiers were organized according to the decimal system: The smallest military unit was a group of 10 (*arban*), then 100 (*zuut*), 1,000 (*mingghan*), and 10,000 (*tumen*), all led by a quartermaster called the *jurtchi* (homelander). Two to five of the tumens were organized into an *ordu* (army), from which we acquired the word "horde"in English.

But despite his clear-headed reform program, he is not remembered in history as punctual administrator. Above all Genghis is known as a brutal commander that utilized psychological warfare for conquest. The reputation is by and large well earned. He avenged the death of his father by obliterating the Tatar tribe responsible and ordering the death of all their males shorter than three feet – a wide scale act of child slaughter. Legend goes that upon defeating the Taichi'ut tribe he boiled the enemy chiefs alive. Upon conquering the khanate of Mongolia, he implemented a policy in which his soldiers ransacked towns to spread fear to the cities. Besieged cities were offered an opportunity to surrender and pay tribute or be destroyed. Those that surrendered were required to support the Mongolian army with supplies or manpower. Those that refused were wiped out, except for a few inhabitants that were instructed to leave and report the destruction to neighboring populations.

Along with a ruthless reputation, Temujin's success was based on a skilled and well-prepared army. He relied on intelligence reports from his extensive spy network. His descendants spent years preparing their conquest of Eastern Europe by gathering reports on topography, the Roman Road network, and populated settlements. His soldiers were well-supplied despite their basic provisions. All soldiers were furnished with full battle equipment, including swords, spears, and shields, along with generous food rations and extra uniforms. The cavalry carried body armor, battle-axes, and a lance. Saddlebags were waterproof and inflatable to prevent drowning on river crossing. The Mongols had complex signal system of torches, smoke signals, and drums. The afterguard consisted of numerous supply wagons, doctors, accounting (for plunder), and even spiritual guides.

Temujin slowly gained control over all of Mongolia; partly through military conquest, partly through diplomacy. After spending a decade consolidating the state by subduing rival clans and tribes under his rule, Genghis Kahn looked beyond Mongolia to China and the Jin Dynasty. This was not due to grandiose dreams of empire building alone, but also for obtaining necessary provisions. The Mongolian steppe was not a fertile location, and the nomadic population was susceptible to starvation.

China was therefore an important target due to its extensive rice fields. When the armies met, the Jin army sent a messenger who promptly defected and gave up intelligence. At Badger Pass, the Mongols killed thousands of the Jin soldiers. They then sacked the Jin capital of Yanjing (modern-day Beijing). The emperor Xuanzong moved south, abandoning the northern part of the kingdom to the Mongols.

An uprising by the already-deposed Naiman Khan Kuchlug, who had fled to Kara-Khitan, was met by Genghis's forces. This was 10 years into the China campaign and the

Mongolian troops were exhausted. He dispatched an army of just 20,000, and rather than attack him in battle, he relied on an uprising by the Kuchlug's troops. By 1218, Kuchlug was captured and executed, thus ending the revolt. The western portion of the Mongolian Empire extended to Lake Balkhash. Genghis now looked over the horizon was the Caspian Sea and Persia, preparing for the next stage of conquest.

The effectiveness of his next stage in conquest owed to his goals being more than simple pillaging and plundering for the sake of money and wives, though he had plenty of both. The goal was always to expand, subdue, and rule. While his army accomplished the initial conquest of new populations, it was through his influence, dominance, and legal reforms that he created peace throughout his empire, a period commonly referred to as the Pax Mongolica. Subjects were to adhere to the Khan's Yasal code, a simple system of egalitarian common law.

According to its statues no one was allowed to participate in any act that would compromise the balance and integrity of the empire, whether the act was as mundane as theft, or as subtle as polluting the water supply. The implementation of this law is an open question, but Genghis at the very least changed legal discourse in his empire. Moral and ethical laws were set, well-known and strictly enforced. Crime was ostensibly not tolerated and if committed was swiftly and brutally punished.

His ability to adapt technology from other cultures was another reason for his success, enabling his army to win against larger opponents. Siege technology borrowed from the Chinese and Persian armies (and implemented on the battlefield by Chinese and Persian engineers who had joined the Mongolian army) allowed the Mongolian army to conquer well-fortified cities. They could build siege engines on the site of battle, rather than disassembling siege engines and carrying them by horses to be rebuilt at the next site as European armies did.

Newly-conquered subjects were allowed religious freedom in his empire, allowing various religious groups to rise high in the military and political hierarchy. Within his court Genghis had Buddhist, Muslim, and even Nestorian Christian advisors, along with concubines of similar faith traditions. Genghis Khan also allowed free trade along the Silk Road and provided security along the route. It opened a travel artery that connected Southeast Asia to Central Europe, planting the seeds for a primitive medieval global economy. This was the route taken by Marco Polo, when from 1271 to 1295 he traveled overland from Italy to the court of Kublai Khan, Ghengis' grandson.

During his 20-year military campaign, much effort was spent on westward expansion. Genghis first attempted to build up a trade relationship with the Turkish Khwarizm. The relationship was quickly destroyed when the governor Otrar captured his diplomats. Genghis demanded that the governor be turned over. When the ruler Shah Muhammad refused, Genghis took personal charge of a planned attack. In 1219, a three-pronged Mongol army of 200,000 turned west. In every town, they completely obliterated the population, taking no prisoners, not even woman, children, or animals. Skulls were stacked in pyramids. The Mongols killed Shah Muhammad, and the dynasty fell in 1221.

When Genghis conquered the Khwarizm Dynasty, he was forced to return eastward and quell an uprising of the Tanguts of Xi Xia. They refused to participate in his westward campaign and began revolting. Genghis Kahn and his army campaigned against the Tanguts city by city until the conquest of the capital, Ning Hia. As a warning to any others considering revolt, he executed the entire imperial family.

Shortly after yet another glorious conquest, Genghis Khan met an ignominious end. The commander who had conquered all of Asia up to the borders of the Middle Eastern states died not from a battle injury or enemy fire but from injuries sustained after falling off a horse during a hunting accident. His generals were shocked, imagining it to be retribution from the Gods. Following the custom of his ancestors, he was buried in an unmarked grave.

Genghis had the foresight to appoint his successor before death to prevent a civil war among his sons. His designated heir Ogedei gained the lion's share of his domains, while the rest of his empire was divided among his other sons. They expanded his conquests and pushed the domains of the Mongolian Empire from Korea in the east to Hungary in the west and Russia in the north. At its maximum extent it was the largest empire in history, four times larger than Alexander the Great's and eight times larger than the Rome.

Such great accomplishments were made possible by the deaths of millions of peasant unfortunate enough to be caught under his military might. Historians estimate that during his reign, Genghis Khan and his armies were responsible for some 10 million deaths. The high death toll was due to his conquest policy of handing over the conquered women and children to his soldiers and slaughtering the rest. In his western campaigns he eliminated three-fourths of the population of the Iranian plateau, which it did not regain until the 20th century. In the capture of the city of Urgench, medieval historians estimate 1.2 million people were killed. His immediate descendants would go on to kill another 30 million, resulting in the carbon offsetting scheme we saw at the beginning of this chapter.

Genghis Khan showed at a very young age how brutal and resilient he could be. More importantly, he was a visionary leader who saw potential in the populations of the Mongolia steppe. He grasped the importance of establishing alliances and laws. His military acumen afforded him insight not only into the battlefield but the needs of each soldier. This vision vaulted his empire far beyond traditional Mongolian borders into the far reaches of Eurasia, leaving behind a legacy of legal reform, trade, conquest, and brutality.

Despite his descendants crushing the Middle East, Ghengis Khan is still respected by Muslims today as a world conqueror. Ghengis remains a popular boy's name in Turkey and other Central Asian countries, and he is a favored mascot of Middle Eastern restaurants. He even occupies a special place in Islamic history and is considered a true world conqueror blessed by God and matched only by Alexander the Great and Timur the Tatar. In the Middle

Ages, countless Muslim rulers aspired to match Ghengis Khan's conquests, believing that one who attained similar levels of success would be appointed by God to conquer the world and usher in the end times.

Genghis was also a popular figure with the fairer sex, producing countless children through his many wives and concubines. In 2003 an international team of geneticists announced after a 10-year survey that one out of every 200 men on earth are directly descended from Genghis Khan. In the domains of the former Mongolian Empire that number rises to one in eight. His numerous descendants are the result of him fathering countless children and his sons continuing the practice.

His first-born son Jochi had 40 legitimate sons; his grandson Kublai Khan had 22 sons. All of his immediate descendants were prominent Middle Eastern and Central Asian rulers in their own right, and their progeny could immediately claim prestige as a ruler by showing their connection to Genghis, thus prompting many aristocratic women and princesses to bear their children and gain access to the power of belonging to his bloodline.

His power was so far reaching that it extended out from his military command and today lives in the blood of his millions of descendants and even in the carbon record of Planet Earth.

Chapter 6

John Churchill, Duke of Marlborough (1650-1722): Master Strategist, Hero of the War of Spanish Succession

John Churchill, the 1st Duke of Marlborough, was a brilliant strategist and a master politician; fortunate for him because if he had not been both, he may not have succeeded at either. He rose from relatively obscure beginnings to become one of the most successful commanders of Enlightenment-era Europe and commander-in-chief of England in the War of Spanish Succession. He was loyal to the British throne but always kept its occupant in mind in order to succor enough political support for his military goals. He was a power broker as part of the Triumvirate that served Queen Anne along with Robert Hartley and Sidney Godolphin. Although he did not revolutionize the design of warfare in the early modern period, his lasting legacy is permanently altering Britain's political trajectory.

His descendant Winston, the bulldog prime minister that led Britain through World War II, lauded his descendant with the highest adulations possible: "He commanded the armies of Europe against France for ten campaigns. He fought four great battles and many important actions...He never fought a battle that he did not win, nor besieged a fortress that he did not take...He quitted war invincible: and no sooner was his guiding hand withdrawn than disaster overtook the armies he had led. Successive generations have not ceased to name him with Hannibal and Caesar."

Marlborough was born on May 24, 1650. His father, also named Winston, was a member of Parliament. Although not wealthy, the elder Churchill was a royalist who held significant influence with Charles II due to his loyalty during the English Civil War. He used his connections to obtain for his sons positions in prestigious schools and the military.

John was educated at St. Paul's school in London and later at Court where he served as a page to the Duke of York, the future James II. John married Sarah Jennings, a woman in a similarly precarious financial position who was also blessed to be in the company of power. She was an attendant to Princess Anne, the future Queen. Marlborough was able to rise on his own laurels, but his wife's influence with Queen Anne secured his military and political power.

Following Marlborough's tenure as page to James, Duke of York, he received a commission as an ensign in 1667 in the King's Company. This was likely due to the influence of his sister Arabella, who was the duke's mistress. He then served three years in Tangiers, where he received practical training in strategy and tactics as the British kept the Moors at bay. He returned to London three years later to serve with James in the Anglo-Dutch war, specifically on the Duke's flagship at the Battle of Solebay as a member of the First Guards. This was a ferocious battle resulting in the British and Dutch each losing 2,000 men. Both sides declared victory, although history has declared it a stalemate.

The result for Marlborough was more positive. He was commended for his skills and promoted to captain in the Admiralty Regiment. He took part in the siege of Maastricht, where he was part of a 30-man force that successfully captured and defended part of the fortress. During this incident he saved the Duke of Monmouth's life in the battle. He was then made a Colonel of the English in service to Louis XIV and commended by the king for his deed. In 1674, he was once again recognized for his leadership at the battle of Enzheim and in 1675 at the battle of Sasbach, where Turenne was killed.

His military genius became evident quickly. Through his command he architected English victories in battlefields across Europe, which had been torn apart by warfare between Catholicism and Protestantism in the course of the Thirty Years War. He had a far-reaching ability to grasp broad military issues on the local, national, and international levels; military historians credit him with seeing the entirety of the Spanish Succession war from its beginnings. He preferred battle to slow-moving siege warfare and was an expert at assessing his enemy's characteristics in battle. His battlefield was a chessboard in which he brilliantly maneuvered his soldiers and artillery, tactically disrupting his opponents. Marlborough coordinated the movement of troops, fire, and all-arms attacks in a complex but efficient manner.

Marlborough was also an expert logistician. He maintained strong supply lines for soldiers while fighting abroad, securing for them necessary arms, clothing, and food even while deep in hostile enemy territory. When armies arrived at their destination they found the supply apparatus operational and the necessary goods for them to wage war already awaiting them. Such quotidian actions earned the trust of his soldiers for showing concern for their welfare and praise from officers for being a man of humanity.

To fill out his resume, he was a political genius and master statesman. Marlborough held together a political alliance against France due to willpower, self-discipline and stamina. He also navigated the treacherous waters of the battle for the British throne, throwing his support behind the winning factions. The first such test came in 1685 when James II, a Roman Catholic, became king. He was not well-received among English Protestants; James Scott, First Duke of Monmouth immediately challenged him for the throne, and rebellion broke out. King James appointed Marlborough as second-in-command of the army appointed to quell the rebellion. With the Earl of Feversham in overall command, he was able to pursue Monmouth's makeshift army of rebels, finally defeating them at the battle of Sedgemoor. Marlborough was promoted to Major General.

His diplomatic ability to stay ahead of the intrigues of the Royal Court and military were tested in the Glorious Revolution. In 1688, James II's reign end prematurely as his mainly-Protestant subjects increasingly resisted his promotion of Catholicism among his court and society at large. Marlborough stayed loyal to James, but even his support was somewhat tenuous. He firmly reminded the king of his personal allegiance to his Protestant faith and that he would not convert to Catholicism, unlike many others at his court. Marlborough saw that James's reign would likely end soon and looked for a means to disassociate himself from the king and his diminishing fortunes.

A group of officials wrote a letter to William, Prince of Orange, pledging their support to the Protestant royal should he claim the throne. Marlborough was not among the signatories, but he sent messages William informing him that he supported the plan and that "it has pleased God to give you both the will and the power to protect."

When William finally invaded Torbay accompanied by a Dutch and English force, the now Lieutenant-General Marlborough was once again second-in-command to Feversham in defending the crown. Yet he openly encouraged defection among the ranks and eventually left himself, slipping away with 400 men. He wrote to the king that he was activated by a higher principle. While he would always give his life to protect the person of the king and he laws, he would not support his reign. James II realized that without Marlborough, his chances for holding the throne were non-existent. He abdicated and fled for France.

William of Orange ascended the throne as William III and ruled in consort with Mary, James II's eldest daughter. Marlborough's assurances of allegiance to a Protestant monarchy and to William were met with some suspicion, but he was rewarded for siding with the new monarch against James and was appointed the Earl of Marlborough, a member of the Privy Council, and kept his military rank. He immediately set out to reorganize the military, including officer appointments, which gave him a great deal of political clout.

William joined in the campaign to thwart King Louis XIV's ambitions for the conquest of Europe. He desired to destroy Europe's most powerful nation and strike the French king, whose reputation with showering himself in obscene levels of wealth was richly deserved. As England was still a regional powerful and not able to defeat France by means of its own resources, he assembled an alliance with the Netherlands, the Holy Roman Empire, Spain, Portugal,

Sweden, and the Duchy of Savoy; thus creating the Grand Alliance.

Marlborough was not in command of any large assault forces during the Nine Year's War, also known as the War of the Grand Alliance; he was left to protect the English mainland. He did earn distinction in the War in Flanders, where he impressed Prince Waldeck, the commander of the allied troops, by commanding the 8,000 British troops to victory at the 1689 Battle of Walcourt in Spanish Netherlands. Marlborough also led his first independent campaign in Ireland in 1690, where he captured the towns of Cork and Kinsale. The Irish were sympathetic to the possibility of James returning as king and Marlborough sought to root out any remaining rebel forces.

The shaky relationship between Marlborough and King William continued to deteriorate, particularly for he and his wife's influence on Princess Anne, a potential rival to the throne. In 1691, he was stripped of all his appointments. The following year he was accused of being part of a plot to return James II to the throne. The charges were unfounded, for although Marlborough had been in correspondence with James, this was an accepted and understandable political practice. The treason charges stemmed from a phony letter of which Marlborough was allegedly a signatory. He was imprisoned in the Tower of London for six weeks but released when the evidence against him was found to be weak. He was then accused of warning the French of an imminent attack at Brest. Again, the evidence that he warned the French was not strong: Most likely, he wrote a letter to James II after the plans were already known. Nonetheless, his fortunes had not turned. Along with his own misfortunes, his wife Sarah had suffered a falling out with Queen Mary, who demanded that Princess Anne break off her relationship with Sarah.

Queen Mary died in 1695, which helped Marlborough ease tensions with William. Yet he did not receive back his appointments and was implicated in another conspiracy. This plot was created by Joseph Fenwick, a James loyalist who was eventually caught and executed. Finally, in 1698

Marlborough was given back his Privy Council and his military appointments. He was appointed governor to the Duke of Gloucester. His famed military career was finally ready to begin in earnest.

Despite his suspicions of Marlborough, William confirmed his confidence in him as a military leader when he gave him command in a campaign to stop Louis XIV. When King Charles II of Spain died childless in 1700, the last of the Spanish Habsburg Dynasty, it set off the War of Spanish Succession as Charles appointed Louis XIV's grandson as his successor, which would have united Spain and France, creating a massive global power that would have dwarfed the other European states. When William died later that year, Anne, who was now queen, re-affirmed Marlborough's appointment. He went to Europe as part of the Grand Alliance of those opposing Louis XIV along with the Dutch and the Holy Roman Empire.

Marlborough led the British, Dutch, and other alliance forces in battle. But his skills as a statesman were tested in order to keep the heterogeneous army operational: He only had command of Dutch forces while they fought alongside the English. He had to seek Dutch government permission for moving and commanding them independently during times of non-combat. This was granted when Marlborough's mettle was proven to be of worthy quality. He quickly and successfully captured the area between the Rhine and Meuse rivers, a strategic point to move their forces.

In 1704, he needed to deploy his army to the Danube to assist the Austrians, who were threatened by the French from the West. France sought to knock out the Holy Roman Empire out of the war by capturing Vienna. He wanted to march on the capital city to protect it but knew that the Dutch would never approve such a long-distance march for its troops or anything that would weaken their forces in Spanish Netherlands. But he also needed to keep Austria in the war and push back France's eastern armies. It is here on the Blenheim that he launched the most audacious, deceptive, and successful plan of his military career.

Marlborough masterminded a plan of movement and

disinformation to intercept the French and Bavarian forces before reaching Vienna. In order to confuse them of his true intentions, he marched with 40,000 soldiers to the Danube, pretending to campaign on the French city of Moselle. This was a massive logistical operation, as it required shifting his army from the Netherlands to the Danube in only five weeks. It was dubbed the dawn of modern warfare, due to the amount of planning and procuring the necessary equipment. He also deceived the enemy by feigning an attack of Strasbourg. Marlborough even ordered bridges to be constructed across the Rhine to further confuse the French.

After uniting with Prussian and Danish forces, he linked up with the princes of Savoy and Baden, forming an army of 110,000. He finally encountered the Franco-Bavarian forces along the Danube near the banks of the Blenheim. The French army was arranged in a four-mile long stretch from the Danube north to the woods of Swabia Jura. They attacked Blenheim on August 13.

The attacks were initially unsuccessful but the French commander Clérambault made a massive blunder by panicking and ordering in reserves into the village. The overall French commander Tallards was depleted of his reserves. Marlborough saw his advantage and pressed it, flanking and pinning down Tallards. He was able to defeat the cavalry and route the French infantry. They and the Bavarians fled. Clérambault's remaining force of 10,000 in Blenheim surrendered.

In the aftermath of the battle, the Grand Alliance suffered 4,500 fatalities and 8,000 casualties, a massive amount, but only one-third that of their opponents. The French suffered 20,000 deaths and 15,000 forces captured. Bavaria was out of the war, the French threat of Vienna ended, and Louis XIV now realized it needed to prepare for a long war. It was the war's turning point and the unofficial end of France's military dominance over Europe.

Now a national hero, Marlborough gained further victories at Trier and Tribach. These victories not only pushed the French further back, but also raised Marlborough's profile on the continent. He was given the

Principality of Mindelheim by the Holy Roman Emperor as a reward for his success. The Dutch and Spanish commended him. But being a hero in multiple countries came with a price. Leading the Grand Alliance meant further embroilment in politics at home and abroad, particularly at a time when support for the war waned. The Whigs were politically ascendant and not convinced that the war was worth the effort. Queen Anne and Sarah's relationship ran into a rough patch due to Sarah's rather strong opinions and tactlessness.

His allies were also dragging their feet in the final stages of the War of Succession. When he saw an opportunity to attack the French and bring a decisive end to hostilities, the Dutch were reluctant to follow. This is despite the war taking place in their homeland, such as the 1705 Battle of Reinheim. Despite tepid support he continued to rack up victories; In 1706 he handily defeated the French near Ramillies. His army of 60,000 nearly suffered defeat when Dutch squadrons were routed by a French attack, but he regained momentum by leading two charges in which the cavalry cut down enemy horsemen and the French center. The Allies only lost 1,000 soldiers; the French 13,000.

At home, the political situation worsened. He had been allied in Parliament with Tory Robert Hartley, but he was replaced due to the growing power of the Whigs. Marlborough had to align with them in order for the government to continue funding the war. In the midst of all this, Queen Anne finally had a split with her former confidant Sarah and thereby severed Marlborough's connection to the crown.

The French dug in and refused to surrender. The Alliance saw cracks form as members such as Sweden considered attacking its allies to gain power. Marlborough, ever the statesmen, kept the allies in line and maintained the Whigs begrudging support for the war. The tide turned once again in their favor in 1708 when Marlborough won a major victory at the Battle of Oudenaarde. Nevertheless, a treaty still could not be negotiated, especially with the Whig demand for a French abandonment of its claims to the Spanish throne.

King Louis refused.

At the battle of Malplaquet he defeated the French once again, albeit losing 25,000 troops to their 12,000. It was a victory but not a resounding one. In 1710, peace talks began again, but the French were still not ready to concede. Marlborough had one more major battle to win to force French capitulation. In 1711 he met French commander Villars, who was present at Malplaquet, at Avesnes-le-Comte-Arras. Rather than facing the forces directly, he executed a brilliant surprise attack on their army through a secret march. His troops covered 40 miles in 18 hours. They took the fortress of Bouchain with a small loss of life.

In the final stages of war Marlborough was forced to tend to domestic issues. He was accused of corruption and embezzlement during his command for issuing a 2.5% levy on the pay of all foreign contingents in the army. The accusations against him were likely political posturing and a means to dismiss the most visible figure in an increasingly unpopular war since he had spent the levy on the Secret Service. Queen Anne was no longer his patron and she dismissed him as head of the military.

Following this humiliating turn of events, he left England and washed his hands clean of its politics, returning to the European continent with Sarah. Here he was welcomed with open arms. The Holy Roman Empire made him a prince and gave him sovereignty of Mindelheim in southern Germany. The French as well were relieved that he was no longer in command and continued to drag out negotiations.

Although Marlborough was not in England, he was never far from England's politics, as he worked towards integrating the German House of Hanover into the line of English succession upon the death of Queen Anne. He kept in contact with her as well, and although the contents of their correspondence are not known, it appears that he reconciled with her at the end of his life, as he was invited to return to England. Marlborough arrived home on the day of her death. He was able to acquire back most of his appointments. He even oversaw one final military campaign and presided over the defeat of the 1715 Catholic Jacobite uprising by those who wanted a return of the House of Stuart to the throne.

The Duke of Marlborough retired to Blenheim Palace, which was still under construction. He was unfortunately only able to enjoy it for three years. His health was fading, and in In May 1716 he suffered a stroke, leaving him mentally clear but verbally impaired. He suffered a second stroke in 1722, leading to his death on June 16. He died in Windsor Lodge at the age of 72.

Marlborough lived in a time of intrigue for the British throne, where factions continually usurped one another in order to gain power. He showed brilliance in navigating these fierce waters, keeping an eye on the throne's current occupant one and future occupants as well. He was an ambitious and brilliant military commander who demonstrated military acumen and also changed the political fortunes of Britain. After commanding his country to victory in the War of Spanish Succession, Britain became a major military power in Europe.

It is a role that it has not relinquished since, even though it was done by a man so thoroughly maligned and misunderstood in his lifetime.

Chapter 7:

Frederick II of Prussia (1712-1786): Patron Saint of Tactical Genius, Forefather of the German Empire

In 1730 the crown prince of Prussia was fleeing for his life to England under the cover of darkness. The young 18-year-old travelled with his tutor, Hans Hermann von Katte, and a group of young army officers. They likely would have arrived safely to England had not a brother of the prince's companions ratted out the group when then were near Mannheim in the Electorate of the Palatinate. The young son was forcibly returned to his father's court and his tutor executed. He himself was court-martialed by his father and could have been executed if not for the intervention of the Holy Roman Emperor Charles VI, claiming that a prince could only be tried by the Imperial Diet of the Holy Roman Empire itself. He was imprisoned for two months and then exiled for the court for another six.

This was the relationship that Frederick II had with his father, Fredrick William I of Prussia. The elder Frederick was a strict disciplinarian of the highest order, training his son to be a soldier from birth. The younger Frederick was awoken each morning with the sound of cannon fire. He was given a regiment of children to instruct and drill at the age of 6, and later that year given a miniature arsenal. The king instructed his son's tutors to beat him if he was thrown off a charging horse or committing such effect actions as wearing gloves in the winter.

The young prince, though, preferred a life of quiet study. He contented himself with music, the arts, French philosophy, and thousands of volumes of Greek and Latin poetry. This unconventional mindset, however, is possibly the source of Frederick II's towering success as a military leader and transformer of imperial Prussia. He reformed the state bureaucracy and civil service. He fancied himself an enlightened absolutist and promoted religious tolerance among Catholics, Protestants, and Jews. He promoted the arts and patronized such court musicians as C.P.E Bach and Johann Joachim Quantz. Frederick aspired to be a philosopher king in the mold of Plato's *The Republic* and the life of Marcus Aurelius. He endorsed the philosophical underpinnings of the French Enlightenment and kept-up a long term correspondence with Voltaire.

All of these attributes stood in contrast to his father, a soldier-king that created the massive war machine of Prussia but did not promulgate a unified culture or rich civil society in the messy collection of small principalities that made up his domains. It had an enormous army of 200,000 soldiers but not a common national identity. It is for this reason that Prussia under the reign of his father, and into the reign of Frederick II, was described by Minister Friedrich von Schrötter as "not a country with an army, but an army with a country."

Frederick the younger did not desire a soldier or general's life, but when circumstance and the man met, he embraced his new role as few did before. He was given a superior army and took full advantage of it, embodying what some have described as "the utmost in military achievement that was possible in Europe in the conditions prevailing before the French revolution." He knew how to defeat superior numbers with superior troops and superior tactics. He also knew when to replace belligerence with diplomacy. Although he took up this career reluctantly, Frederick built a legacy that lives on today in modern German.

Frederick was born in 1712 in Potsdam, near Berlin. He was the oldest son of Frederick William I of Prussia and Princess Sophie. Following his failed attempt to flee Prussia, his father decided not to execute Frederick, but did execute Von Katte while his son was forced to watch. Frederick was pardoned but lost his military rank. He was also forced to acquire the education in military and statecraft that he had been avoiding in the past.

Frederick returned to Berlin two years later. In 1733 he

agreed to marry Elisabeth Christine of Brunswick-Beven, a relative of the Austrian Habsburgs, , after avoiding previous attempts at arranged marriages. Elisabeth was devoted to him, but he was not happy to marry her; so much so that there were loud whispers among his court that the marriage was never consummated.

Despite his troubled nuptials, he enjoyed the early years of his reign. Frederick passed the time watching plays, enjoying music, and continuing his study of French literature, even beginning a correspondence with Voltaire. He also wrote books, in particular a refutation of "The Prince" entitled *Anti-Machievel*. Frederick's thesis stated that the concepts described in the classic primer of power politics were no longer relevant in the 18th century. He fully grasped the political change that had taken place in Europe as it transitioned from the city-states of Machiavelli's age to the small number of powerful states and empires of Frederick's age.

In addition to his intellectual pursuits, he became dedicated to his work in government, thereby impressed his father. He also rejoined the military and was appointed commandant of an infantry regiment. Frederick was part of Prussian contingent that assisted Austria in the War of Polish Succession. In this capacity, he served under the very successful Prince Eugene of Savoy in his campaign against the French. Additionally, he founded the Bayard Order, a group that studied military issues.

In 1740, Frederick William died and Frederick II ascended the Prussian throne. Shortly afterward, Emperor Charles VI of Austria also died. Prior to his death, Charles pondered deeply over his choice of successor, as he worried that his daughter and heir, Maria Theresa, would not be accepted as the legitimate heir to the throne. Hapsburg dynastic law did not accept a female as the ruling monarch, but Charles VI lacked a son and had no other choice. To avoid any belligerence, he created the Pragmatic Sanction of 1713, which allowed the hereditary possessions of the Hasburgs to be inherited by a daughter.

However, France and Bavaria both had designs on

Austria, as did Frederick. They were all eager for a political environment in which a weakened Habsburg empire could not defend its valuable lands. Frederick let it be known to Maria Theresa that he was willing to assist her in military matters, but his cooperation would come at a price. He demanded that in exchange for such cooperation the Province of Silesia become incorporated into Prussia. When Maria Theresa refused, he declared war on Austria, a conflict which became known as the Austrian War of Secession.

In order to wage a war considered legitimate in the international arena, Fredrick used the 1537 Treaty of Brieg as a pretense. It stated that the Hohenzollerns of Brandenburg – a royal Prussian family that included the emperors – were to inherit the Duchy of Brieg, located in Hapsburg lands. The excuse was considered to be sufficient by neighboring states also eager to carve out portions of the Holy Roman Empire. He was joined in the war by France and Bavaria.

The Prussian Army was not battle tested, but was the most skilled and best-trained army in Europe. He inherited a standing army of 83,000 men; when he died it rose to 190,000. The army recruited peasants from the countryside and paid them by taxing townsmen that in turn were exempted from military service. Furthermore, he prevented nobles from interfering in military matters, creating a more personal link between the national army and the conscript. No longer were nobles the filter through which military reforms occurred; in 1749 and 1764 he issued decrees that limited the obligations of a peasant to his lord.

Fredrick's first command experience was in the Battle of Mollwitz in 1741, where he defeated the Austrians. The Prussian cavalry performed poorly at first, but the cuirassiers, originally trained on heavy horses, were retrained on more maneuverable and lighter horses. Following this victory, he turned and attacked the Austrians once again at the Battle of Choyusitz after falling back. Once again, the Prussian soldiers' skills had turned the tide. Frederick reached an agreement with Theresa Marie and withdrew from the war in 1742, having obtained most of Silesia. However, Austria became much more formidable without Prussia in the war. Realizing that this could have adverse implications for both Prussia and its new possession, Frederick decided to resume Prussia's participation in the conflict. The war ended in 1748 with the Treaty of Aix-la-Chapelle. Austria had managed to hold onto all its domains from its encircling neighbors, with the exception of Silsea.

The European nations were suspect of Frederick's next intentions for conquest and further expansion across the continent. Russia, Austria, France, Saxony, and Sweden all united against him. Austria and France, which had traditionally been enemies, now formed an alliance. Frederick, concerned for Prussia's security, entered into an alliance with Britain and the House of Hanover at the Convention of Westminster. In 1756, he invaded Saxony and thus started the Seven Year War.

Frederick held a numerical disadvantage in the war but was still able to succeed due to the superiority training of his troops, which prevailed time after time in battle. Frederick also used superior tactics against his much larger enemy. He would not give the nations that composed the alliance an opportunity to combine their forces while on march and launch a unified attack. Thus he mitigated the alliance's strength in numbers by attacking with a smaller but more skilled army. His army travelled in smaller units and would combine forces immediately before a battle. Additionally, his opponents' reliance on traditional battle formations exposed their vulnerabilities.

Frederick inspired his troops through his personal involvement in battle. Like Alexander, Hannibal, and Khalid ibn al-Walif before him, he frequently led his military forces into combat. As a result, six horses were shot out from under him into battle over the course of his career.

His bravery and tactical brilliance earned him a reputation as a genius, particularly for his use of the "oblique" order of battle, a military tactic in which an attacking army focuses its forces on a single enemy flank. His army targeted the enemy's weak point, using the remainder of its forces to fix the enemy line. One he effectively punched a hole in their defenses, his army would then create an angled formation with a concentration of force. They could envelop the flank and defeat the enemy in detail. It was often through this method that he attained victory with smaller forces on the battlefield.

Executing this order required three things. First, precise formation was necessary. Each officer needed to know how to form a battalion from line to column, maintain its place in the column, and then redeploy normally or en echelon for an attack. Second, the soldiers had to march in formation, in step. This required structured formations. Lastly, his enemies could not be aware of the formation, since it could be countered with a quick response. All of these requirements were difficult for one commander to execute, but not for Frederick, who was an aficionado of details and skilled in the art of subterfuge.

The masterpiece of his military career came December 5, 1757, at the Battle of Leuthen. He had recently won a victory over the French at Rossbach on November 5, which secured Prussia against a French invasion. He now turned to the powerful Austrian force under the command of Prince Charles of Lorraine. At Frederick's command were 35,000 men, 133 squadrons of cavalry, 78 heavy guns, and 98 battalion field pieces. The men under his command were confident after victory, but another half of his force who had fought under a different commander were demoralized after a strategic retreat from Breslau. This was the sum of his force that he had to attack the Austrian army at Silesia, which possessed 85 battalions, 125 squadrons, 235 guns, and 60,000 troops. They were a highly professional force that had three times defeated the Prussians in battle.

He first set out to raise his men's spirits. Although sick and exhausted, he joined the troops and warmed himself at the men's fires, listening to their stories, hearing complaints, and promising rewards and promotion for valiant service. He showed camaraderie to senior officers and inspired them instead of belittling them: "Bear in mind, gentlemen, that we shall be fighting for our glory, the preservation of our homes, and for our wives and children," he said. With these words he instilled in them utmost confidence that they would achieve victory. To further raise their spirits, he issued an increased ration of food and liquor.

Frederick knew that there were Austrian positions near Breslau, which was held with 1,000 Croats and two regiments. His first action was to drive them out before a larger force came to occupy it, thereby preventing them from placing infantry in the town and artillery on the hills. This robbed the Austrians of a strong position. He took Breslau by having a portion of his forces batter down the town's gate, followed by a cavalry regiment charging into the city. A third regiment entered by Breslau's back gate, surprising the Austrians. In total, 800 Croats were captured. The Prussian army then advanced and occupied villages in the immediate area.

According to his intelligence, the Austrian army created a four-mile-long defensive line near the village of Nippern. His plan of attack went in the following order: First the army was preceded by an advance guard of 60 squadrons and 10 battalions, led by Frederick himself. Four columns of the army followed behind, with the infantry forming the two middle columns and the cavalry the wings. His advanced guard was the first to encounter the Austrian advanced cavalry guard, which was not part of the main army. Frederick ordered his cavalry to charge the Austrian front with the full support of the infantry. This force routed the Austrians, forcing them to flee back to the main Austrian army. Over 800 Austrian infantrymen and five officers were captured.

He continued the Prussian advance until they were in sight of the Austrian army. It was plainly visible before him, and he could discern all its strengths and weaknesses. He saw the chink in their battle formations: a knoll upon which the left flank was anchored, from which the ground sloped downward. If this could be captured, then his army would have an advantage throughout the battle. To conceal his movements to the south, Frederick used the terrain to hide his soldiers and ordered a portion of his army to go through a show of deploying into battle order in the north, fooling them of his real intentions.

He successfully executed his maneuver and prepared for attack by arranging the oblique order on the Austrian southern flank. The attack force was supported by a battery of 12-pounders. Frederick's left flank, which had been used to confuse the Austrians, supported a cavalry force that would guard against a Prussian retreat if the first attack failed.

The Prussians quickly captured the knoll, giving them a favorable position over the entire Leuthian plain. They prevented an Austrian counterattack by placing a battery of their artillery on the knoll. They made slow progress, but soon the Austrian cavalry was forced into retreat. They were forced from their initial positions and fell back on the village of Leuthen. The Austrians attacked to change their position and form a new line parallel to the Prussian front.

The Prussians entered Lethuan and the focus of the battle now centered around a churchyard surrounded by a tall stone wall. They took the church, and the Austrians remaining in the town were driven north. They attempted one more counterattack outside of the town against the Prussians. But Frederick ordered his left flank to attack the Austrian right. The latter were dispersed and fled in disorder. They soon came under attack from three sides. With this assault, Prussian victory had been won. They suffered a total 6,382 casualties; The Austrians 10,000 casualties and 12,000 captured. Additionally, 131 Austrian guns were captured.

Despite this glorious victory, time was not on Frederick's side. The alliance was strong enough to drain his resources and threaten Prussia with bankruptcy. Russia had also invaded Berlin, putting more pressure on him for a swift resolution. However, his fortunes changed when Empress Elizabeth died and was replaced by Peter III. The new Russian ruler had no desire to continue the war with Prussia. In 1763, the war was settled in the Peace of Hubertusberg, with Prussia maintaining its pre-war territory.

Although he did not acquire any new land in the war, Frederick did gain insight concerning the next necessary steps to make Prussia a dominant political and military force in the Concert of Europe. This would take more than superior battle tactics or training; it would take diplomacy. He would also have to change his first-strike policy and rely more on the defense of his domains. He signed a defensive alliance with Empress Catherine II of Russia, who had taken over the throne after her husband Peter had been assassinated. Despite mutual mistrust, the alliance was effective, as both monarchs were pragmatists to the core.

The alliance was tested when Russia entered into war with the Ottoman Empire in 1768. Frederick was concerned with Russia's growing power, as its intention in the war was to bring the Caucasus and the Crimea into its orbit, adding Ottoman lands to its domains. Frederick's brother, Henry, proposed that it make its own land grab by seizing Poland and partitioning it between Prussia, Russia, and Austria. Frederick captured this area and quickly set about to assimilate it into his domains. He renamed the new territory West Prussia. He required that his ministers learn Polish, even though he showed outward contempt for the new province. He encouraged German people to move to this acquired territory and reform the education system. The plan worked: as many as 300,000 Germans settled in West Prussia and made a tremendous impact on the land's culture and society.

When Joseph II of Austria chose to invade Bavaria, Frederick used diplomacy and various threats to pressured him not to follow through. Joseph moved ahead anyway, and Frederick was drawn halfheartedly into the conflict. He prepared his forces for battle, but nothing occurred beyond a minor skirmish. The conflict ended with the Treaty of Teschen. Austria received Burgau and Prussia received the Franconian principalities. The other result of the treaty was the creation of the League of German Princes, which was formed to protect Germans against outside forces.

Frederick's strengths went far beyond his strengths as a military leader. He demanded hard work and loyalty from his appointees, which led to effective governance. He filled the coffers of the treasury despite expensive military expansion by creating an effective tax system that was the envy of Europe. He also built up Prussia's industrial base so that his state could manufacture its own primitive goods. Ironically, one area in which he did not develop Prussian society was in art and literature, particularly in light of his personal appreciation of high culture.

In his later years Frederick grew more solitary. He became less interested in fraternizing with the population of Berlin and instead preferred to retreat within his estates. The circle of friends that he maintained throughout his life at the royal court died off and younger members did not replace them. He grew critical and arbitrary of those around him, much to the annoyance of high ranking officials and bureaucrats. His condition worsened, and in 1786, he died at the palace of Sanssouci in his beloved study. He was entombed next to his father in the Potsdam Garrison church.

In his 46-year-resign, Frederick promoted Prussia from a small state to the top tier of European powers. He doubled its land size and made it the dominant force in the German states. Such actions eventually led to the unification of Prussia's princely states into unified German nation in 1871, built on the groundwork that he had laid. Primary education and the codification of law occurred under his reign. He transformed the military from an aristocratic institution to a feature of society that was relevant to all social classes, whether it was the noblemen leading the army, the middle class supplying the army, or the peasants that made up its rank-and-file soldiers.

Perhaps the greatest compliment to his reigns comes from an equally ambitious military commander that also vaulted his nation to new levels of power. Mere decades after Frederick's death, an influential French commander paid homage to the Prussian ruler and boasted that the latter was the greatest tactical genius of all time. Following a stunning victory in 1807, the commander took pilgrimage to his tomb in Postdam, paying his respects to the unofficial patron saint of unexpected military conquest.

Standing in front of Frederick's grave, Napoleon Bonaparte remarked to his officers, "Gentlemen, if this man were still alive, I would not be here."

Chapter 8

Alexander Suvorov (1729-1800): Russia's Sun Tzu; Conqueror of the Turks, French, and Polish

This Russian general, the only commander capable of stopping Napoleon's advance across Europe in the 18th century and successfully defeating his generals, is a repository of quotes and wisdom that have influenced generations of military commanders. In his *Science of Victory*, he crafted a treatise on the essential morale, training, and initiative of front-line soldiers. It was written for the Russian peasants that formed the core of his army for the purpose of recasting them as proper soldiers. Alexander Suvorov is a complex figure, but his philosophy is perhaps best encapsulated in his remark that to win, one must train hard and fight easy.

In this regard Suvorov was a sterling example to his troops. He fought almost 100 battles and won every single one. They were obtained by his unconventional strategies and fierce disciplining of his troops. He furthermore accomplished these goals while avoiding the decadent culture of Moscow. Suvorov had no use for the obsequious flattery to the czars that defined military leadership in 18th-century Imperial Russia. In a time when military leaders were often more interested in the comforts of aristocratic life, he generally ignored court intrigue in favor of the battlefield. The only people whom he sought to earn their respect were the soldiers under his command, with which he shared the same level of material comfort.

Suvorov was born in Moscow in 1730. His father, Vasily Suvorov, was a general-in-chief, or full general, in the Russian army, as well as a senator. His mother was Armenian. He was a sickly child and his father had little faith that his son would achieve any significant level of success; he was therefore only fit for a civil service position. However, the young Suvorov worked hard to become of sound of mind and body, overcoming the limiting beliefs that his father had placed upon him. He taught himself four languages and studied military history, strategy, and tactics using his father's vast library. He engaged in rigorous physical exercise to strengthen his constitution. His dedicated efforts impressed his grandfather, General Gannibal, so much so that he convinced Vasily to let his son pursue a career in the military. At 18, Suvorov joined the army and attended classes at Cadet Corps of Land Forces. He spent six years in the Semyonovsky Life Guard Regiment.

His first battle was part of the Seven Years War against Prussia, which took place from 1756-1763. By this time, all doubts about his abilities had been laid to rest. Suvorov was commended for his performance in the field and promoted to colonel. It was at this point that his career truly took off, due to the 1762 enthronement of Empress Catherine the Great. Suvorov was assigned a commission in Poland, where an uprising was taking place in the Confederate of the Bar. He defeated General Pulaski's army, conquering Krakow. The war was the prelude to the first partition of Poland, which split the country between Russia, Austria, and Prussia. Once the campaign cease, he was promoted to major-general.

In the course of these battles Suvorov implemented battle tactics that he had personally crafted. These maneuvers eschewed complex drills and emphasized a more basic approach that relied on precision, aggression, and direct assault. It was an unconventional approach, but bold and effective against enemy forces. He also emphasized a rapid attack over patience. "Judgment of eye, speed and attack are the basis of victory," he commented.

Suvorov's next major campaign was in the Russo-Turkish War of 1768-1774, fought against the Ottoman Empire, the arch-enemy of the Russians. He did not join the war until 1773, but his influence was decisive. His victories over the Ottoman army earned established his reputation as an extraordinary field commander and leader. However, his disdain for politics and adherence to the government became manifestly apparent. He launched unauthorized actions against the Turks and was therefore tried and sentenced to death. Despite his churlish attitude toward politicking the royal family, his military successes earned the favor of the equally militaristic Empress Catherine II. She did not uphold the verdict and stated that winners cannot be judged.

In 1774, after treaty negotiations broke down, he took command against the Ottoman army at the Battle of Kozluca. The Turks had an overwhelming numerical advantage with 40,000 troops. However, the Russians were able to overtake them with superior firepower and by dividing and conquering the Ottoman forces. In this battle he caught part of the Turkish army attempting to cross a Danube tributary. His fierce assault on their rear flank overwhelmed the Ottomans and drove them back on the main army, creating an opportunity for the Russians to overrun their encampment. The Russians only suffered 200 casualties to the Ottomans' 3,000. Due to this loss they surrendered much of the Black Sea's northern coast, turning it into a Russian lake. The war ended shortly after and he was promoted to lieutenant-general.

Known as "The Soldier's General," Suvorov had earned a reputation for many aspects of his character. He respected his troops by ensuring that they were properly paid and equipped, not an easy matter in a time of primitive bureaucracy and courier-based communications networks.

Suvorov's writings make him a repository of quotes on military matters, something of a Russian Sun Tzu. He believed in attacking at the earliest opportunity rather than tarry in favor of perfect circumstances; or, as he more eloquently stated, "attack with what comes up, with what God sends." Although he did not believe in the Prussian zealous approach to all things military, he did believe in thorough discipline of his soldiers, or that "a hard drill makes an easy battle."

Other armies increasingly relied on battlefield artillery to break down the enemy, but Suvorov had greater confidence in the bayonet and hand-to-hand combat. Rifles in the 18th century took a considerably time to reload, sometimes up to a full minute, so he ordered his troops to bayonet the first enemy they encountered and shoot the second. "The bullet is a mad thing; only the bayonet knows what it is about," he commented in "The Science of Victory."

He trained them to fighting with speed and mobility, accuracy of fire and the bayonet, all within a carefully executed strategy that he personally oversaw. W. Lyon Blease notes in the biography of Suvorov that he himself was comfortable with an operational scheme that granted him complete power and control over the smallest decision: "The officers know that I myself am not ashamed to work at this. ...Suvorov was Major, and Adjutant, and everything down to Corporal; I myself looked into everything and could teach everybody."

His determination is the primary reason for never losing a battle. Unlike other contemporary generals that had enjoyed great military success, Suvorov never considered retreat to be a viable strategic option. His reluctance of retreat was not for fear of punishment; rather, it was a means to instill confidence in his troops that victory was never impossible. His third reason for success was limiting the number of officers, resulting in a more efficient military machine with fewer intermediaries between top generals and front-line soldiers. Suvorov abandoned drills and communicated to his troops in a clear manner. Similar to the logistically-minded generals of the past such as Frederick the Great and Marlborough, he saw to his soldiers' overall well-being by taking care of the army's supply lines and living conditions. This resulted in far lower rates of illness in the army camps.

After victories in smaller skirmishes, Suvorov took command in the Russo-Turkish War of 1787-1792. He was victorious at the battle of Ochakov and Kinburn. At Kinburn in 1787 the Turks attempted to stop the Russian fleet and prevent a siege of Ochakov. As the Ottomans attacked, Suvorov launched a counterattack and benefitted when the shells from the Turkish navy's own fleet landed on them. In the offensive strike, Suvorov was injured twice. He did not mind the injury, as it was part of his pursuit of the retreating Turkish soldiers. With this episode in mind, he is quoted in Savkin's "Basic Principles of Operational Art and Tactics" that, "A strong pursuit, gives no time for the enemy to think, takes advantage of victory, uproots him, and cuts off his escape route."

The final casualties of the battle totaled 400 for the Russians and 4,000 for the Ottomans. The war continued, and in 1790, he attacked the fortress of Ismail at Bessarabia on the Danube River, among his most famous victories. The fortress was thought to be impenetrable due to its size, yet the Russians successfully stormed it. The Turkish soldiers had orders to stand their ground and declined the Russian ultimatum to surrender. This was seen as his military masterpiece, a catastrophic defeat for the Ottomans, and the tipping point in the war. The victory was a glorious moment and immortalized in Russia's first national anthem. For his service during the war, Catherine the Great rewarded him with the victory title *Rymniksky*.

In 1794 Suvorov was called upon to crush the Polish uprising. At the Battle of Maciejowice, the Russians were able to attack before the Polish reinforcements arrived. It was a swift and brutal campaign, and the Polish commander Taduesz Kosciuszko was captured. The Russians then stormed the Warsaw and neighboring Praga. During the attack on Praga, Cossacks killed 20,000 civilians. There is some question as to whether these Cossacks were under Suvorov's command in the course of their slaughter of victims. Nonetheless, he is partially responsible for the atrocity, as he did allow the Cossack's an extended period to plunder the city.

The campaign garnered him a reputation as a ruthless and brutal commander in Europe, as many civilians were killed in the collateral damage of the city's plundering. According to Suvorov's military calculus, however, it was a justified order. A violent but rapid finish to a war would result in far less loss of human life than a more gentlemanly but protracted military conflict. "It is very difficult to do one's duty. I was considered a barbarian because at the storming of the Praga 7,000 people were killed. Europe says that I am a monster. I myself have read this in the papers, but I would have liked to talk to people about this and ask them: is it not better to finish a war with the death of 7,000 people rather than to drag it on and kill 100,000?"

When the war finished and Warsaw was captured, he expressed his joy to the Empress in his characteristically steely manner. He sent this simple message to Catherine: "Hurrah, from Warsaw, Suvorov."

After the Polish campaign concluded, the 64-year-old commander retired to his estate at Konchansko. Just as he had done so with his soldiers, he lived on the same level as the townspeople and worked alongside them in their farming duties. Shortly after his retirement, Catherine died in 1796 and her son Paul I became czar. Suvorov had become critical of the army, and Paul cut him and the entire military off from his inner circle. Unlike his mother, his personality was not amenable to the general; Paul preferred all the pomp and circumstance of drills and parades, which made Suvorov's toes curl. The old general quickly fell out of favor with the royal court and was dismissed. However, Paul experienced an abrupt change of heart when the first Napoleonic war began, threatening the independence of Russia. Suvorov was recruited to lead the defense of Italy in 1798.

Russia joined with Austria in an alliance against France to drive them out of Italy. Suvorov prepared his troops and was appointed Field Marshall by Austrian Emperor Franz. He arrived in northern Italy while Napoleon Bonaparte was busy fighting in Egypt. His combined army of 45,000 troops won victories at Cassano d'Adda, Trebbia, and Novi. In the first two, he bested French Generals Jean Moreau and Etienne MacDonald. At Novi, Suvorov executed his battle tactics that he had spent his career perfecting. The French commander, Barthelemy Catherine Joubert, was killed in the opening moments of the battle. The last victory essentially expelled French forces from Italy.

Nonetheless, Austrian and Great Britain feared for his position in southern Europe, as it gave him an excellent platform to attack the heart of the continent. They called for

Suvorov to march to Switzerland and reinforce the Austrian armies rather than march directly to France. Ammunition and supplies promised by the Austrians had not been delivered, so he had to attack French troops with limited supplies while holding the St. Gotthard Pass, the quickest but most difficult route to Switzerland. He broke through the French position after he had outflanked them and charged them three times. On September 25, he outflanked and attacked the French again, who were attempted to hold the Lucerne-Lach tunnel and the Devil's Bridge. Suvorov stepped onto the bridge himself during the battle and called to his army "See how an old field marshal faces the enemy!"

However, a second Russian army had been defeated in Zurich and Suvorov had no means to ferry his army across the lake there. The French were closing in on their Alpine position and the Russians feared they were trapped. They had no reinforcements and limited supplies. Time was running out.

In order to evade the French forces once again, Suvorov ordered an Alpine expedition that was reminiscent of Hannibal and his trek that took place two millennia earlier. He ordered his army to march into the 9,000-foot-high mounts of the Panikh range towards the Ilands in order to reach the Upper Rhine. The Russians had to negotiate this difficult passage while conceding the French the higher and better vantage points. Nonetheless, the Russians, never afraid to endure the most brutal elements of the cold, successfully traversed the snow-covered Alps despite suffering continual attacks. Against all reasonable expectation, he managed this treacherous strategic retreat. He lost one-third of his army but gained the respect of Europe's elite for executing it successfully. For his victory, the elderly Suvorov was give the top rank of Generalissimo of Russia, the fourth and last holder of the title in pre-Revolutionary Russia.

Suvorov returned to St. Petersburg in 1800, but sadly not to a hero's welcome. Paul had promised a victory celebration but Suvorov's command, rank, and titles were instead stripped away due to a suspected misdemeanor of military administration. The general was heartbroken and worn out from a lifetime of battle. Retirement did not suit him well, as he was listless without his *raison d'etre* of commanding military forces.

Furthermore, his military career had created deep tensions with his family, above all with his wife. He was not an affectionate husband, nor did he attempt to compensate for his long absences with any sort of romantic gestures: Suvorov once wrote a letter to her that only stated "Alive. In health. Serving. Suvorov." She in returned was widely rumored to have engaged in numerous affairs while he was away on military campaigns. The life to which he returned offered him little incentive to continue living. He died on May 18 of the same year. Befitting his utilitarian manner, the inscription on his gravestone merely states, "Here lies Suvorov."

The general had built up a record of 93 victories in battle and zero defeats, virtually unmatched in history. It owed to his steely resolve, single-minded determination, and ascetic lifestyle. He was able to win against superior numbers. His strategy left no room for retreat. When he went to war, he did not take advantage of any special privilege, but lived as a common soldier, thus building excellent camaraderie and trust with troops in the front line. His frugal style was legendary, as he preferred to live a camp-like lifestyle even when away from the battlefield, sleeping on hay and shunning blankets in cold weather. One legend goes that Catherine ordered him to wear a fur coat that had been offered and rejected by him. In order to follow her order yet keep to his habits, he carried the coat without putting it on.

However, his open distaste for politics perhaps limited the speed of his rise in the military chain of command. As we discussed in the introduction to this book, many of history's most famous generals were black sheep whose brilliance also made them outliers and poor at the elbow rubbing necessary to navigate the world of elite diplomacy. But whatever political acumen he lacked, his military brilliance ensured at least cordial relations with Tsarina Catherine and, to a lesser extent, her son Paul.

His ability to move forces on the chessboard of the battlefield was unparalleled in his time. At the operational level, he concentrated forces to destroy the enemy's supply lines and strike the enemy's weakest point. He emphasized the mobilization of small forces rather than large, lumbering regiments. Suvorov sent units into battle piecemeal to maintain momentum against the enemy, enabling a mobile army that could quickly shift positions to delivered a blow to the enemy's vulnerable positions and create a sustained attack.

Perhaps the highest esteem that honors his memory comes from the Order of Suvorov, a military decoration of the Russian Federation awarded to outstanding senior personnel. The 40mm-wide gold-plated cross pattée is awarded to those demonstrating exceptional leadership in combat operations and skilled organization of troops and military units despite stubborn resistance of the enemy.

Among military historians and the Russian people, his reputation as a commander was second to none. The man whose father thought he would never amount to anything proved indispensable to his country.

Chapter 9

Napoleon Bonaparte (1769-1821): Emperor of France, Ruler of Europe, Exile of Elba

In 1798 Napoleon landed his forces in Egypt, which at the time was an Ottoman province. The purpose of the campaign was ostensibly to protect French trade interests; undermine Britain's access to India, its most lucrative colony; and establish a scientific enterprise in the region. Concerning the last count, it was by any metric a rousing success. His expedition included a contingent of 167 scientists and scholars. The Rosetta Stone was discovered, which unlocked Egyptian hieroglyphics and opened up the ancient past to generations of researchers, founding the science of Egyptology. The printing press was introduced to a wider population and made possible newspapers and journals in French and Arabic. Ideas such as nationalism and liberalism were promulgated. Other Enlightenment values were propagated in Egypt through the founding of the Institut d'Égypte, a learned academy that carried out research during the expedition. His scholars also observed the regions' flora and fauna and its other natural resources.

Conversely, whatever his devotion to Enlightenment principles, many military historians believe the true reason of bringing along the contingent of *savants* was to hide his actual motives of invasion: to increase France's power and prepare for conquest of the European continent. And Napoleon could behave boorishly in cross-cultural contexts. He had certain mosques transformed into cafes and ordered that the tricolor flag be flown from minarets. Civil officials often did not acquiesce to these boorish commands, causing at least five or six heads to roll off the guillotine each day. The situation of the French deteriorated the longer they stayed in Egypt. His callous attitude toward the locals earned him deep scorn, and they didn't care about whatever military power or Enlightenment attitudes he possessed.

Thus are the contradictions embedded in a man widely considered to be among the greatest commanders in history. He challenged the *ancien* regimes of Europe and permanently altered the political order of the continent, placing multiple nations on a trajectory toward democratic rule and civil rights. Yet he did so by assuming untold-levels of autocratic power and running roughshod over his opponents. His megalomanic tendencies made him disinterested in the suffering and death of his soldiers; he was only interested in their contribution to his aggrandizement, and that was all that truly mattered to him. In the end, his political ambitions bankrupted France and permanently consigned it to a second-tier status among the colonial heavyweights of 19th-century Europe.

His greatest lasting legacies were battlefield strategies copied by Europe's national armies from the late 18th century until the invention of the rifled musket in the mid-19th century. The core of his tactics relied on a highly efficient military machine. It required the intense drilling of soldiers, speedy battlefield movement, combined arms assaults between infantry, cavalry, and artillery, bayonet charges, short-ranged flintlock musket fire, and a small number of cannons. The invention of the rifled musket made such strategies technologically impractical, but it was Napoleon who invented this strategy and attained its apotheosis. He preferred a flexibly used of artillery, which required marching in columns instead of lines. This made maximal use of the short range muskets, and it mowed down enemy lines.

Napoleon was born in 1769 at Ajaccio on the island of Corsica. He was the son of Carlo Bounaparte, a lawyer, and Letizia Romalino Bounaparte. His family was considered among the Corsican elite, although they were not wealthy. France had recently acquired Corsica from the Italian city-state of Genoa. Napoleon attended school in France, where he learned the language and attended military academies at Brienne and Parisian Ecole Royal Miltaire, graduating in

1785. He was appointed as a second lieutenant in the French Army artillery unit. His father died the same year.

He could not have come of age at a more exciting time in France. The Revolution began in 1789; within three years, the government was overthrown, King Louis XVI was dead, and the French Republic was born. Bonaparte worked to spread the Revolution's ideals to his home island. He spent much of the first eight years of his officer's appointment in Corsica, taking part in local politics. He joined a pro-democracy group and aligned with a former patron of his father, Pasquale Paoli, governor of Corsica. He also was involved with the revolutionary Jacobin faction and became a lieutenant colonel in the Corsican militia.

Following the optimism of the Revolution, there came a dark chapter in France's history, known as the Reign of Terror. Maximilien de Robespierre, the leader of the revolution, used "universal compulsory force" to kill all those who did not agree with the extremist aims of a French Republic. As a result, he and Jacobin sympathizers used the guillotine to kill nobles, clerics, and anyone who had a hint of political opposition. Supporters marched through the streets of Paris with the heads of decapitated priests on the end of pikes. The Reign of Terror that reached its nadir with the 1793 executions of Louis XVI and Marie Antoinette, and it would not end until Robespierre's execution.

During this turmoil Napoleon was appointed to captain in the French army, despite his extended time away from the country. In 1793, his allegiance to the governor ended when Paoli attempted to gain Corsican independence from France. Napoleon and his mother left for the French mainland and Gallicized their name to "Bonaparte."

He was tasked with quelling an uprising at Toulon, which was occupied by British troops and the French that were revolting against the Reign of Terror. Napoleon devised a plan to capture republican artillery located at Point l'Eguillete and dominate the city's harbor, forcing the British naval forces to evacuate. They did as such, and the pro-republican French were left defenseless. Napoleon was wounded in the thigh during the assault, but his command in battle earned him a special commendation. He was promoted to Brigadier General and caught the attention of Augustin Robespierre, brother of Maximilien. This relationship was critical to his future career, even if it was short-lived, due to Robespierre's death in 1794.

Napoleon quelled another revolt in 1795, this time of counter-revolutionaries and Royalist in Paris, lining up artillery to stop the attack. For quelling the revolt, he was rewarded by the French Directory, France's governing body, and gained a new patron in its leader, Paul Barras. Shortly afterwards, he married Josephine de Beauharnais.

The young officer rose through the ranks of the French army, largely owed to his remarkable intellectual ability and power of memory. One story from his campaign of 1805 claimed that a subordinate of his could not locate his division, and his aids search through maps and papers to assist him. The emperor told the officer his unit's present location, where he would be station for the next three nights, his unit's strength, and the subordinate's military record. This was despite the subordinates being one of 200,000 soldiers, with units constantly on the move.

Napoleon later in his career boasted that his extensive study of military history and devouring of hundreds of volumes made him a fully formed battle commander before he ever ordered any troops to attack. He once claimed, "I have fought sixty battles and I have learned nothing which I did not know at the beginning. Look at Caesar; he fought the first like the last."

In 1796, Napoleon commanded the first of his international campaigns in Italy. He took over a poorly equipped and exhausted army that was completely dispirited. They were, however, an experienced group, and Napoleon was able to turn around their fortunes by properly supplying the troops. More importantly, he gave them better incentives for victory.

In this campaign Napoleon had to fight two battle-hardened armies: the Austrian and the Piedmont. His first objective was to keep the two armies separated by prevent their armies from uniting at Carcare, specifically by exploiting the reluctance of the Piedmont army. As he readied for battle, the Austrians, led by General Beaulieu, decided to attack first. The French were able to prevail and defeat them at Dega. Eventually, the Piedmont troops agreed to an armistice after retreating westward.

He was now able to prepare an attack on the Austrian army, which he chased across the Po Valley. He defeated them at Lodi by preventing their retreat. This was followed by his capture of Milan. These victories helped solidify his reputation as a commander capable of leading international campaigns. Napoleon then drove the Austrians out of the Lombardy. With Italy defenseless, he conquered the Papal states and seized Venice, ultimately extracting over 60 million francs in plunder.

Napoleon introduced many innovations in this battle. He used the army corps as a replacement for the division as the army's main organization. Each of these corps was something of a miniature army consisting of infantry, artillery, and cavalry. It only numbered 10,000 to 30,000 and was a flexible arrangement compared to the lumbering juggernauts that made up Europe's other armies. Such an arrangement could hold off a larger army until help arrived. The entire army did not need to march together; therefore, military logistics were far simpler and allowed for surprise attacks against the enemy. Each of the different corps could quickly come to the aid of another in battle, or quickly exploit a weakness in the enemy's lines. The principle was to march divided and to fight united.

He faced a stronger united force to test the effectiveness of his army's organization. Austrian Field Marshal Count von Wurmer's forced arrived to unite with Beaulieu's army. The Austrians had initial success with an attack on a garrison near Brescia. However, Napoleon counterattacked swiftly and successfully, winning the Battle of Lonato and the Battle of Castiglone. The French defeated the outnumbered Austrians at the Battle of Bassano; they subsequently retreated to Mantua. They finally surrendered after losing the Battle of Ravioli and realizing that they would not be sent reinforcements. Filled with enthusiasm and possible delusions of grandeur that pushed him to overstep the bounds of his rank, Napoleon authorized the terms of surrender in the Treaty of Campo Formio despite lacking the authority to do so. However, the French Directors agreed to the terms, which included taking control of the Austrian-controlled Netherlands and the conquered portions of Italy. The French also took control of the Holy Roman Empire.

In 1798, the Five Directors had considered invading England, but Napoleon convinced them to invade Egypt and cut off English trade routes instead. Napoleon defeated the Mamluks, a provincial Ottoman-backed dynasty who essentially ruled Egypt, at the Battle of the Pyramids. Unfortunately, he found that his concerns with the British were correct when his fleet was defeated by the Royal Navy on the Nile. He also invaded Syria to gain control over the Ottoman Empire but was unsuccessful in his siege of Acre.

Without receiving orders to do so, Napoleon decided to return to France after he saw that his replacement had lost northern Italy in the War of the Second Coalition. He and the Directory had become concerned about an invasion of France; however, its fortunes had reversed once again before his return when its border security was restored.. Nonetheless, the country was bankrupt and the popularity of the Directory was waning. Napoleon was unquestionably the most popular figure in the country due to his meteoric rise and sterling military career. He was recruited by one of the Directors, Emmanuel Joseph Sieyes, to overthrow the government.

Bonaparte was placed in charge of protecting the legislative councils and convinced them to relocate to the Chateau de Saint-Cloud for safety. In fact, they were being pushed out of the way for a council assembled by Bonaparte and Sieyes, also the chief political theorist of the French Revolution. He thought that he would become France's leader, but Napoleon was able to maneuver into being elected as First Consul. He assumed legal power as well and wrote the Constitution of the Year VIII. The general from Corsica was now the leader of France.

Napoleon instituted drastic and far-reaching reforms to

French government, which had already transformed considerably in the previous two decades. He created a centralized banking system, a university system, tax reforms, and public works. He also created the Napoleonic Code, which institutionalized many ideas of the French Revolution by weakening the power of the aristocracy and feudal tradition. It removed birthright privileges, established freedom of religion in the Catholic-dominated country, and established career placement in the government bureaucracy based on merit. This legal code was created by second consul Jean Jacques Regis de Cambaceres, along with major influence from Bonaparte himself.

Napoleon also reconciled his state's extremist secular tendencies with the Papacy. During the Revolution, a push for secularism coincided with the desire to destroy the influence of the Catholic church in society. Although Napoleon himself was not religious, the overwhelming majority of the French were Catholic. He negotiated a Concordant that improved relations while at the same time theoretically it gave him more influence in the Church within France.

Regarding his innovations that he brought to the battlefield, three main military strategies undergirded Napoleon's battle philosophy, as noted by Peter Dean. The first was la maneuver sur les derrieres, in which the enemy was pinned by a feint attack and then the army marched by a hidden rout to attack the enemy's rear flank. It took his enemies more than a decade to learn of a countermeasure. The second was to favor a central position when encountering two or more enemy armies. This allowed him to engage each enemy separately, thus defeating more powerful forces. During the Waterloo campaign Napoleon was able to attack Blucher's Prussians while Marshal Ney's corps dealt with Wellington's Anglo-Dutch army. The third maneuver was strategic penetration. This involved smashing of the enemy's corridor of defenses, followed by a rapid march deep into enemy territory to seize a city or town and use it as the base of operations for the next step of the campaign.

Napoleon returned to Italy in 1800 to once again defeat the Austrians. After the battle of Marengo, the Austrians were completely driven out of Italy. He reached a peace agreement with the British when they signed the Treaty of Amiens in 1801, as both nations had tired of war. In the Western Hemisphere, however, the French faced an unexpected uprising in the African slave-dominated island Haiti in 1803. Napoleon decided that defending any French territory in North America would be almost impossible; he resolved to sell the Louisiana Territory to the United States, thus filling his treasury and preventing his resources from being overextended across the globe.

In 1804, a plot by the House of Bourbon was uncovered to assassinate Napoleon. He decided to prevent any claimants to the throne from challenging his rule by creating his own line of succession and appointing himself emperor. Napoleon was crowned as such at an elaborate ceremony at Notre Dame du Paris with Pope Pius VII present and had his Josephine crowned as empress. The pope had been promised Italy in return for his blessing, but Napoleon reneged, declaring himself King of Italy the following year.

Napoleon decided that the time had come to attack Britain. They were reluctant to fight after the disastrous 1799-1802 War of the Second Coalition but realized the danger that the French emperor posed to the rest of the continent. They formed the Fifth Coalition with Russia and Austria. Napoleon knew that he could not cross the English Channel and directly attack the powerful British Navy, but he believed he could lure them away and attack far from their home bases. He planned to cross the Channel and attack while the British fleet was otherwise occupied. His plan failed utterly, as he knew little of naval strategy or of the resources required to launch a successful amphibious attack. The British won a decisive victory at the Battle of Trafalgar and establish superiority on the seas.

On the continent, Napoleon's fortunes fared much better. It is here in 1806 that many military historians consider to be the apogee of his military career. He defeated the Austrians and Ulm at the Battle of Austerlitz, also known as the Battle of Three Emperors, and forced the Austrians to once again surrender. Before the battle, Napoleon was not confident in his ability to defeat the large coalition forces consisting of a Russo-Austrian arm, commanded by Tsar Alexander I and Holy Roman Emperor Francis II. He could only muster 72,000 men and 157 guns, while the allies had 85,000 troops and 318 guns. The Allies planned to use their superior forces to strike France's right flank and launch a diversionary attack against the left. The tsar threw his support behind this plan and stripped Russian commander-in-chief Kutuzov of authority, giving it to Austrian Chief of Staff Franz von Weyrother.

Napoleon crafted a brilliant plan to counter this strategy. He shrugged off all suggestions from his marshals for retreat and lured the Alliance to attack on his right flank by deliberately weakening it. This would cause the Allied forces to leave vulnerable the Pratzen Heights in order to move to the right side. He would then launch a surprise counterattack in the center by concealing his forces in a dead ground opposite the Pratzen Heights. His troops would attack and recapture the Heights, then launch an assault on the center of the Allied Army, deliver a debilitating strike, and encircle them from the rear.

The first allied column attacked the village of Telnitz, where the French 3rd Line Regiment was pushed back but held the line and launched counterattacks. They were eventually joined by reinforcements and pushed the Allies out of Telnitz. The Allied columns launched their assault on the French right in a slow and poorly coordinated attack. As they continued on the French's right, Kutuzov's IV Corp stopped at the Pratzen Heights and remained there, understanding its importance for the battle. The tsar, however, did not and ordered the IV Corp from the Heights. This created the opening that France required for a victory.

Napoleon ordered the attack on the heights at 9 a.m. In a dense fog, General Louis de Saint-Hilaire led his division up the slopes. They emerged from the fog, much to the surprise of the Russian soldiers. The Allies quickly moved columns over to fend off against this offensive maneuver; this unit was quickly destroyed. Hilaire's men bayoneted them out of the Heights.

On the north end of the battlefield, the Allies were being defeated at Stare Vinohrady by French General Dominique Vandamme. He broke several Allied battalions. The Russians pushed forward in a desperate charge led by the Russian Imperial Guard, commanded by Grand Duke Constantine, Tsar Alexander's brother. Napoleon's heavy guard repelled the attack. The Russians were finally forced to retreat. Their line was broken and the horse artillery of the Guard inflicted heavy casualties upon them, and slaughtered many in their retreat. At the northern end of the battle, the French lighter cavalry, led by Francois Kellerman, successfully halted the Austrian advance of Prince Liechenstein and the Russian infantry.

The final stage of the battle came. Napoleon's forces shifted to the southern part of the battlefield. The French and Allies continued to fight over Sokolnitz and Telnitz. In a double-pronged assault, St. Hilaire's division and Davout's III Corps broke the line at Sokolnitz. The first two columns of the Allied forces fled. The Allied army was now in full panic and abandoned the field. In one possibly apocryphal tale, the Russians who had been defeated by the French right flank attempted to withdraw to Vienna by running over the frozen Satschan ponds. As French artillery exploded around them, the ice was broken. As many as 2,000 Russians drowned in the icy waters, although some were rescued by their French adversaries.

The French had defeated the Allies and ended the Third Coalition. In the aftermath of the battle, 27,000 of the Allies' army of 73,000 suffered casualties. They lost 180 guns and 50 standards. The French lost 9,000 out of 67,000 troops. France secured an amazing victory despite teetering on the brink of financial collapse days before. Tsar Alexander commented on the battle with the following lamentation: "We are babies in the hands of a giant." As a result of the aftermath, the Holy Roman Emperor abdicated, the millennium-old empire ceased to exist, and the Confederation of the Rhine, a buffer zone of states between

France and Germany, was created.

To once again attempt to counter Napoleon, a Fourth Coalition was formed among the European states. Fresh off his impressive victory, the French emperor was determined to conquer Europe, consequences be damned. He defeated the Prussians at the Battle of Jena-Auerstedt. This was followed by a push into Poland where the French clashed with the Russians, who were advancing westward. After brutal fighting in the Battle of Ella, a treaty was negotiated between Tsar Alexander I that divided Europe between the two powers.

Napoleon decided that he would counter England's influence with an economic attack in the form of a boycott, which was named the "Continental System." Also known as the Continental Blockade, this foreign policy effected a large-scale embargo against British trade in 1806, as a response to the naval blockade of French coasts enacted by the British government. Among the participants were France's satellite states and occupied zones: Spain, Italy, Austria, Prussia, Switzerland, Sweden, Norway, Finland, and Russia. This system hurt the British, but also damaged the French economy, which was reliant on the former's imports. It was abandoned by Russia and Portugal in 1807 due to the crippling effects of the embargo on their economies. Napoleon asked Spain to join in retaliation against Portugal, but when Spain refused, he ordered his army to attack the entire Iberian Peninsula, in what became the Peninsula War. The French army fought to a stalemate until Napoleon himself joined the fray. France defeated Spain, Portugal, and its allies from Britain. He then declared his brother Joseph the king of Spain. As Spain attempted to retaliate, Austria broke its treaty with France, and Napoleon returned home. The loose-knit empire that had been built in the early stages of the Napoleonic Wars was beginning to come undone.

In 1809, Austria aligned with Britain, forcing Napoleon to take command of his army. In the course of the brutal fighting at Aspern-Essling, he was barely able to fight to a draw, despite his superior numbers. He was able to prevail at the Battle of Wagram, but his resources were dwindling.

Napoleon attempted to shore up political support wherever it could be found, and this included marriage alliances. He had previously divorced Josephine because she could not deliver him an heir and married Austrian Archduchess Marie Louise, Duchess of Parma, in 1810. Yet, while creating one alliance, another difficult relationship became even worse. He annexed the Papal States after the Pope Pius VII refused to endorse his Continental System. The pope responded by excommunicating him. In turn, Napoleon's forces kidnapped the pope, holding him captive for five years.

Throughout all his battles, Napoleon often managed to secure victory through his tremendous force of personality. His enormous confidence enabled him to inspire others, and he knew of the impact that morale had on warfare. Napoleon said that, "morale is to the physical as three is to one." To accomplish this, he secure his troops' loyalty by commanding their obedience to his charismatic person and the revolutionary principles of merit, talent, and elections among peers for promotion, rather than the old corps that served the old nobility and an abstract concept of aristocracy.

At this point in his career, Napoleon's weaknesses as a military commander became more evident. His obsession with military affairs turned him into a micromanager. He promoted men who had flourished under his command but operated poorly as independent officers. Napoleon's inability to keep other European powers divided or adapt to the more violent nature of warfare in the early nineteenth century led to his eventual downfall.

Napoleon had enjoyed a good relationship with Czar Alexander of Russia, but by 1811 it began to unravel due to pressure from the Russian aristocracy and secret diplomatic efforts across Europe that were designed to bring down the French emperor. In April 1812, Britain, Russia and Sweden signed secret agreements against Napoleon. The Russians amassed a huge army along the Polish border numbering 300,000. Napoleon brought his enormous Grand Armee to the Russian border and decided to invade in June of 1812 at the height of his military power. Estimates of his troop strength indicated that he had over a half a million men.

Unlike his brilliant and dynamic victory at Austerlitz, he was now involved in a miserable war of retreat and attrition. Napoleon had been warned against attacking the vast Russian interior, but he saw this conquest as the next step in establishing his empire. The Russians were led by Mikhail Bogdanovich Barclay de Tolly. They initially battled the French, but after some losses they retreated further into the interior, destroying crops and livestock as they moved to cut off the French supply chain.

By September, Napoleon's huge army was reduced 135,000 due to disease, desertions, and battle casualties. He continued marching on to Moscow, hoping to capture the capitol and win the war. After a brutal battle at Borodino, he arrived there only to find that the Russians had escaped the city and then set it ablaze. In October 1812, he was forced to abandon Russia and slowly marched back towards France, his Grande Army now consisting of only 40,000 soldiers.

On his journey back to Paris, Napoleon was forced to contend with a newly invigorated European alliance. The Sixth Coalition consisted of Prussia, England, Portugal, and Spain. Despite his diminishing fortunes, Napoleon was not ready to abandon his grand strategy. He was able to acquire reinforcements from France and Germany, defeating the alliance at the Battle of Dresden in August 1813. Allied casualties numbered 100,000 to the Napoleon's 30,000. Unfortunately for the emperor, Sweden and Austria joined the alliance afterwards, and he had to continue his retreat after the brutal Battle of Nations.

Napoleon was told by his advisors to abdicate, which he agreed to do so his son could be appointed emperor. This was unacceptable to the allies, and he eventually did so unconditionally. He was exiled to Elba, but returned to France in March of 1815 and reclaimed the throne. For 100 days, he once again held power. He marched his army toward Belgium, where he defeated the Prussian army headed by Gebhard Leberecht von Blucher. He then directed his army towards Waterloo to attack the British army, which was led by the Duke of Wellington.

Napoleon delayed his assault while he waited for the

ground to dry from a rainstorm. This gave time for Blucher's troops to arrive. The reinforcements raised the total number of Allied forces to 100,000 troops compared to Napoleon's 72,000. Aside from the disadvantage in numbers, Napoleon was reportedly not as taciturn of a commander as he had been in the past. His once-revolutionary strategies were now familiar to his opponents, and his flanking maneuvers were no longer capable of delivering the same surprise attacks or rapid victories. When the battle ended and his devastating loss was made manifest, Napoleon's career as Commander and Emperor had finished.

Napoleon abdicated once again and spent his remaining years exiled on the British island of Saint-Helena, over 1,000 miles from the west coast of Africa. Here he wrote his memoirs and suffered under poor treatment from his captors. Many sympathizers spoke of rescue plans of the emperor, but most of these plots took on an outlandish character. Some exiled soldiers from his army that had relocated to Texas wanted to resurrect the Napoleonic Empire in America. Others talked of rescuing him in a primitive submarine. It was all for naught, as his health began to fail due to the harsh treatment of his jailers. According to his autopsy, he ultimately succumbed to stomach cancer. The once-great emperor died on May 5, 1821.

His legacy is so far reaching that it is difficult to summarize, yet it is simple in its power. Napoleon Bonaparte forever changed both the country and the continent in which he lived. As both a brilliant commander and tactician, he established a legal code that is still used to this day; adopted the metric system; terminated the Holy Roman Empire's millennium-long influence on the European continent; implemented religious emancipation; and permanently curtailed the power of the French aristocracy in favor of its citizens. However, what he had not done was achieve his grand strategy of building a French Empire that would control Europe and the Middle East.

His accomplishments in life were nearly unparalleled, but they could never live up to his larger-than-life ambition.

Chapter 10:

Robert E. Lee (1807-1870): Hero of the Confederacy and America's Foremost Gentleman

Whatever laurels of military accomplishment that Robert E. Lee lacked by not leading the Confederate forces to victory over the Union, if nothing else he proved Charles Dickens's dictum to be incorrect that he had never met an American gentleman.

Literary scholar Brad Miner describes Lee as the foremost member of a Guild of Gentlemen, a confederacy of decent fellows that constituted a unique species of American aristocratic life in the mid-19th century. They were men who possessed "country, self-restrained, a nice regard to the rules of etiquette, a command of speech, an elegance of dress, a familiarity with the habits of the leisure class, a respect for appearances, for outside things, and a desire to make the passing moment pleasurable."

Lee was not simply the South's paradigm of chivalry; he was America's as well. As Bertram Wyatt-Borwn writes, he exemplified the "three graves of gentility": sociability, learning, and piety. He was a man willing to fight for what be believed to be right. He was offered command of Union forces, but took command of the Confederate Army of Northern Virginian instead, as his loyalty to his state was greater than his loyalty to his nation (a common sentiment when America the nation was less than a century old).

Lee's own definition of a gentleman was well-rounded and reminiscent of medieval traditions of chivalry. It also influenced by the writings of Sir Walter Scott, who had popularized the romantic notions of the Greeks and the Crusaders in 19th-century high society. These focused on manners, respect to women, military affairs, the ideal understandings of democracy, and romantic oratory. It is worth recounting Lee's own definition of chivalry, as through this we may understand what made him such a formidable military general:

"The gentleman does not needlessly and unnecessarily remind an offender of a wrong he may have committed against him. He cannot only forgive, he can forget; and he strives for that nobleness of self and mildness of character which impart sufficient strength to let the past be but the past. A true man of honor feels humbled himself when he cannot help humbling others."

Lee's pedigree helps to explain his refined character. He was from among America's oldest families and a man of honor in the mold of his fellow Virginian, George Washington. Due to his strong educational foundations, he began his military career by putting his mathematical knowledge to use as an engineer but also served as an infantryman and then officer. When the Civil War erupted, Lee continually demonstrated his strength as a commander against an enemy with superior numbers and resources.

Perhaps he is most famously known for his strategic ability to win seemingly impossible victories in spite of his meager resources. He had incredible foresight in anticipating the actions of his enemies and applying pressure to their weaknesses. Lee kept open a convex front toward the enemy so that reinforcements, transfers, and supplies only needed to travel over short, direct routes. He made use of his numerically smaller army by brilliant uses of field fortifications to maneuver these small forces. If such a group was protected by entrenchments, then it could hold back the larger enemy force while his main body of troops outflanked the enemy. This was a strategy decades ahead of its time and was used to great effect in Antietam, Chancellorsville, Fredericksburg, and Gettysburg.

Lee was born in Stratford Planation, Virginia in 1807. He was the fifth and youngest child of Henry "Lighthorse Harry" Lee, a Revolutionary War hero. By the time the younger Lee was born, however, his father's fortunes had fallen, and he was on the brink of financial ruin due to his recklessness with the family's finances. The family moved to Richmond and the senior Lee left for the West Indies when Robert was 11 in order to escape his creditors. He was never to be seen again.

Lee did well at Alexandria Academy, where he showed aptitude for mathematics and finished his secondary education in only three years. In 1825 he then entered West Point Academy, where he impressed his instructors so much that Lee became the first cadet to achieve the rank of sergeant upon the end of his first year. He graduated second in his class in 1829 and had an exemplary record with no demerits. He was then commissioned as a brevet second lieutenant in the Corps of Engineers, the most prestigious branch of the army, and was assigned to projects in Georgia and Michigan. In 1831 he was ordered to Fortress Monroe on the Virginia Peninsula. While there, he reconnected with and married Mary Custis, the great-granddaughter of George Washington's wife, Martha Custis Washington.

Lee's knowledge and use of fortresses in his battle command came from his first army assignments. He helped plan the construction of Fort Pulaski in Georgia (1829-1831) and Fortress Monroe at Old Point Comfort in Virginia (1831-1834). He was promoted to first lieutenant in September 1836 and spent much of the next four years in St. Louis superintending civil engineering projects, particularly protecting the city's harbor from shifts in the channel of the Mississippi. His knowledge of topography proved useful in his later years as a general when it came to choosing infantry and artillery positions on the battlefield.

His valor showed itself first in the Mexican-American War, which he entered as a staff engineer with the column under Brigadier General John E. Wool. He directed the building and repairing of roads and bridges from San Antonio to Saltillo, Mexico. In 1847 he joined General Winfield Scott as chief engineer to the army of invasion. Scott gave him enormous leeway to take initiative in the amphibious assault against Mexico's Gulf Coast. The general commented that Lee was the "very best soldier that I ever saw in the field."

Lee saw further action at Veracruz, Churubusco, and

Chapultepec. In addition to his battlefield commission, he also operated in the intelligence services. It was Lee who penetrated the enemy's mountainous defensive position around Jalapa. Lee discovered a route through the hills around the Mexican left flank and persuaded Scott to use it while leading the vanguard along the left round. The U.S. Forces won the battle of Cerro Gordo on April 17-18 due to this strategy. He also found a feasible route to attack the enemy when it fell back on another strong position in front of Churubusco by skirting across a maze-like lava bed known as Pedregal. It resulted in a fierce assault against the enemy position and a quick victory. Lee received a brevet promotion to colonel.

After the Mexican War, Lee spent four years at corps headquarters until he was appointed Superintendent of West Point in 1852. He was reluctant to take the position because of the political nature of such an appointment. When he did accept the position, he improved the facilities and added an extra year to the curriculum. Along with this he restored cadet discipline, which he found to be lacking. Upon completing this appointment in 1855, Jefferson Davis sent Lee to Texas where he became second-in-command of the Second Cavalry, formed to increase the size of the force patrolling the vast territories in the Southwest obtained after the Mexican-American War. This tour of duty was mostly uneventful, but it gave Lee command experience, particularly in difficult terrain.

Lee's father-in-law died in 1857. As his executor, he had to clean up a disorganized patchwork of assets and debt. Lee spent a great deal of time riding back between Virginia and Texas sorting out these affairs. During one such trip, he was sent by President James Buchanan to Harpers Ferry, Virginia, to quell a slave insurrection led by abolitionist John Brown at a military arsenal. Lee was able to capture Brown and his followers after he ordered the marines to storm his refuge. Brown was taken into custody, but he became a folk hero among abolitionists, and his arrest added considerable fuel to the smoldering pile of internal tensions in the United States over the issue of slavery. It was one of the last harbingers of the Civil War.

Lee then returned to Texas where he witnessed the secession of the state in February 1861. He surrendered his position in the Second Cavalry and then returned to Virginia under orders from Lt. General Scott. He told Lee off the record that in the event of war, he would be Scott's second-in-command and leader in the field. Following this, the newly-elected Abraham Lincoln offered him the rank of Major General in the Union Army.

Lee was caught between the country he loved, a cause in which was not certain of – Lee had owned half a dozen slaves but emancipated them before the Civil War due to his general dislike of slavery – and the state he called home. He would not attack the South, and he promised to defend Virginia, even though he had written that the secessionist Confederacy violated the principles established by the Founding Fathers, believing that a compromise between the North and South could be reached. Nonetheless, he turned down an offer to defend Washington because of his concern of taking up arms against the Commonwealth.

His allegiance to Virginia and the Southern cause was not mirrored in those of his closest family, almost all who backed the Union cause. But when Virginia seceded from the Union in April of 1861, Lee resigned from the army two days later. On April 21, Virginia Governor John Letcher sent a messenger offering Lee command of the military and naval forces of the state. On May 14, 1861, the Confederate War Department conferred upon him the rank of brigadier general of the Confederate States of America, when Virginia's troops were transferred to the Confederacy.

Lee took command in western Virginia to fight against the Union in a section of the state that was mountainous and filled with pro-North sentiment. Lee was sent to Cheat Mountain, where he battled Union General George McClellan. As he would do in the future, Lee delegated authority to his commanders. He split up his forces into three groups in order to allow his forces flexibility to maneuver the difficult terrain. However, the attack was uncoordinated and Lee was defeated.

His efforts in the west to consolidate the state under the Confederate cause were not successful, and the state eventually split into two: Virginia and West Virginia. Lee returned to Richmond where he became a military advisor to Confederate President Jefferson Davis. The new president then sent him to shore up the South Atlantic coast defenses. He made use of his engineering experience and oversaw the rebuilding of crumbling fronts around Savannah, Georgia, and Richmond, Virginia; a needed action since the Federal navy had captured bays and inlets south of Charleston, allowing them to tighten its blockade on the South. He was quickly summoned back to Richmond in March 1862 when the Union offensive threatened to crush the defense of Tennessee and advance on the Confederate capital.

Lee concluded in 1862 that a defensive position against the Union would lead irrevocably to defeat; the North simply had too many resources and manpower, which would allow them endless attacks and the option for overwhelming force. If nothing else, they would be the inevitable victor in a war of attrition. The only possibility for Confederate victory was to go on the offensive and target weak Union strongholds and critical points in their supply chain. He reinforced the army of Major General Thomas J. "Stonewall" Jackson so that it could achieve victory in the Shenandoah Valley campaign of May-June 1862. His army won a number of tactical victories and diverted the Union offensive away from Richmond, slowing down the Northern Army of the Potomac.

He then led his forces against the Northern Army's advance against the Confederate capital, preparing for a direct clash. This was known as the Peninsula campaign, which culminated in the Battle of Seven Days of June 25-July 1. Lee battled General McClellan, known for his penchant for drilling over actual fighting. He and his commanders attacked aggressively, concentrating their forces on the Union army to compensate for their smaller numbers. Stonewall Jackson and his forces joined them outside of Richmond. They achieved victory but in an undesirable way: the Army of the Potomac was not completely destroyed, the battles were tactical messes, and Confederate casualties were extensive.

Lee continued to be propelled forward by the conviction that a devastating Union loss was necessary for the Confederacy to achieve legitimacy and bring an end to the war. He moved north to battle Union Major General John Pope, leader of the Army of Virginia. Lee broke his army into two commands, one under Stonewall Jackson and Major General James Longstreet. On August 28, Jackson attacked Pope's troops at Brawner Farm and fought to a stalemate. The following day, Pope continued his assault on Jackson's troop, not realizing that Longstreet's troops were taking up position on his right flank. Longstreet's army of 28,000 crushed the Union attack, pushing them back to Bull Run. Pope staunched the bleeding of the devastation by defending his rear guard, but the Union forces continued to retreat. Northern casualties numbered 10,000, compared to 1,300 for the Confederates. The Second Battle of Bull Run was a tremendous victory for the South.

Lee's army seized the momentum and crossed the Potomac River into Maryland on September 5. The war shifted northward, and on September 16, 1862, the two sides met at the Battle of Antietam in Maryland. Lee commanded 34,000 men compared to 71,000 Northern forces and was forced to retreat after two days following the loss of 10,000 soldiers.

Part of the reasons for their losses was that McClellan had gained significant military intelligence from the "Lost Order," a copy of the Confederate army's general movement orders issued by Lee in the Maryland Campaign plans. The order gave details of the movements of the divisions of the Army of Northern Virginia. It was accidentally left behind at a Confederate camp and quickly delivered to the Union command upon its discovery. With this intelligence, McClellan realized that the Southern forces were split and that he could make use of this information by attacking at Antietam. However, he was a cautious general and many military historians believed he did not fully exploit this intelligence out of fears that he was walking into a possible trap.

Lee began to remove his army south to Shenandoah Valley, but McClellan did not pursue. He had in fact only used three quarters of his forces in the battle. The first day of the battle was the bloodiest in American history: Antietam's final tally was 12,100 Union casualties vs. 10,000 Confederate casualties. From a military standpoint, the battle was a draw, but the Union considered it a victory because the South had withdrawal from Northern territory. After the battle, Lincoln made two major decisions: he replaced McClellan with Major General Ambrose Burnside as leader of the Army of the Potomac and announced the Emancipation Proclamation. It was only effected in the North, but it reinforced to both sides of the Civil War that Northern victory would bring about the end of slavery.

Lee received word that McClellan had the documents and, following their retreat back across the Potomac, ordered Stonewall Jackson to march North and join with the main Confederate force. He was now fighting on the tactical defensive. Burnside's troops attacked at Fredericksburg, Virginian on December 13, 1862.

In December 1862, Burnside occupied Falmouth, Virginia, located near Fredericksburg. Lee's army took up arms on the heights above the town. The Union army set up bridges across the Rappahannock River to wage an assault. Burnside used a massive army of 60,000 in a full frontal assault but was only briefly able to break through Stonewall Jackson's left flank. The Union suffered 13,300 casualties to Lee's 4,500. It was a masterstroke of military strategy, but Lee was careful not to embrace victory at the expense of neglecting the South's terrible loss of life. He was reported to have said afterwards, "It is well that war is so terrible, or we should grow too fond of it."

Union General Joseph Hooker then took command and led an attack on Lee's left flank at Chancellorsville on May 2-4, 1863. In response, Lee and Jackson crafted a strategy to attack the Union's right flank, which was not protected. Approximately 30,000 Confederate troops swung around the Union forces and attacked from their rear guard. Lee had his remaining front line troops feign attacks to keep the Union forces occupied. Meanwhile, Hooker showed a reluctance to attack. The rebels blasted the Union troops with artillery from the high ground. The Union army was pushed back and attempted a rearguard attack; however, Lee himself went to Salem Church to make sure that victory would be complete. The Union army suffered 18,000 casualties to the Confederate's 13,000. Despite winning his greatest strategic victory, Lee suffered a major casualty when Jackson was shot accidentally by friendly fire. He died from pneumonia weeks later. Hooker's forces were eventually able to break through the Confederate lines, but did not follow through. Hooker lost 13,000 men out of his army of 60,000.

The Confederate army command was now divided as to whether it should push for one last assault on the North or send reinforcements to assist the Confederacy's western armies that were being crushed by Union General Ulysses S. Grant. Lee convinced Davis that another surge to the North was preferable by reasoning that a successful invasion into the North would mean the capture of Union supplies, farmland, and the demoralization of its citizens. To enact this plan, he moved through Maryland to central Pennsylvania. When Lee arrived in Gettysburg, Pennsylvania, he was met by Union forces under the command of General George C. Meade. The Battle of Gettysburg ensued.

On July 1, 1863, the Confederate troops attacked with overwhelming numbers and pushed the Union army directly into Cemetery Hill and Culp Hill on the southern side of the town. It was unfamiliar terrain for Lee and precluded a surprise attack on the enemy flanks. On the second day of the battle, 90,000 Union soldiers defended the hills south of town, while 70,000 Confederates attacked, concentrating on the left flank. The fighting raged and the Confederates gained momentum, but the Union soldiers had successfully held their ground until the day's end.

On the following day, against the advice of General Longstreet, Lee ordered a direct assault against the center of the Union Forces on Cemetery Ridge. It was his last gamble on a major strategic offensive that would destroy the enemy army. This attack, led by General George Pickett – and forever known as Pickett's Charge – was met by a Union artillery barrage. It ended in a Confederate disaster that turned the momentum of battle against them. After once again being defeated in the North, Lee returned to the Confederacy. His army suffered over 28,000 causalities. A third of his officers were wounded, killed, or captured.

Lee's reputation as a strategist and leader was severely damaged at Gettysburg. Much of that had to do with his reputation of using tactics that had become dangerously outdated, causing him to become predictable. Some questioned whether Stonewall Jackson's death prevented him from achieving the successes that the flanking maneuvers led by Jackson in earlier battles had provided. Furthermore, he was ill, and his ability to lead had been diminished. He had always delegated power to his commanders, but their deaths in battle had diminished their ranks and they were replaced with less experienced commanders that could not effectively wield the authority delegated to them.

Lee's inexhaustible belief in the potential of his soldiers inspired them to acts of valor, but their abilities were finite and Lee had pushed his soldiers to the outer limits of their physical and mental capacity. They were not always capable of living up to his grand designs. As a man of honor, he offered to resign his command, but Jefferson Davis refused to accept it. The South was now threatened the eastward advance of General Ulysses S. Grant, its most formidable opponent to date, and a dwindling number of resources. In the spring of 1864 Grant assumed command of the Union army. He was determined to finish the war by wiping out the Army of Northern Virginia, whether through attrition or total destruction.

Grant benefited from his superior troop numbers and North's industrial base, which the South largely lacked, making the Fabian Strategy a reasonable path to victory. He intended to press this advantage until the Confederacy was utterly defeated or exhausted from the two sides trading casualties. Lee had attempted to prevent such an outcome when he waged his first northern campaign but now was faced with such an unwelcome scenario. The momentum of the war had turned hopelessly against him, and Lee was being pushed toward Richmond. In May 1864, the Overland campaign began, and Lee realized that he was battling a new general who was not willing to retreat.

Lee won a tactical victory at the Battle of the Wilderness on May 5-7, at Spotslyvania Courthouse May 7-20, and Cold Harbor on June 3, resulting in 61,000 Union casualties. But Grant kept on pressing south. The Army of Northern Virginian suffered 25,000 casualties, over a third of his 61,000 troops with which he began the campaign. Grant kept Lee's troops fighting on a defensive posture.

Grant attempted to capture Petersburg, Virginia, which was vital to the Confederacy's transportation network and connected Richmond to the lower South. Meade's Army of the Potomac crossed the James River on June 15-16 to attack the railroad junction. His attempt failed and Lee built trenches as a defense for the town, resulting in a deadlock of trench warfare that lasted for months. Petersburg was then put under siege from June 1864 to March 1865.

Lee was down to 44,00 men and could not hold the 20 miles of trenches that surrounded Petersburg against Grant's forces, which numbered 128,000. Lee attempted an assault on the Union Army in order to break through the Federal lines and join forces with General Joseph E. Johnston in the Carolinas. But his assault on Fort Stedman on March 25 failed. Grant finally broke through on April 2, 1865 and shattered Lee's western flank at Five Forks on April 1. Lee abandoned Petersburg. His last stand had failed. All paths of retreat had been closed. Seeing no other viable alternative, he finally surrendered himself and the Army of Northern Virginia to Lee on April 9, 1865 at Appomattox Court House.

Lee's military career in the nascent Confederacy had come to an end. He was indicted for treason by a United States high court, but this indictment was never pursued. However, due to his renouncement of American citizenship at the onset of the war, he lost the right to vote along with his claim to some property. Lee retired, hoping to fall into obscurity.

Nevertheless, his valor and indefatigable defense of the South caused many of its residents to regard him with the deepest of sympathies. Wealthy landowners and politicians offered him a prominent place in Southern society following the conclusion of the war. He was made president of Washington College, a respected institution that had fallen into disrepair after its library and buildings were looted in 1864. It lacked proper funding and a significant student body. Lee, ever the commander, set about to restore the school's status as a beacon of higher education in the south. By the end of his tenure, its enrollment numbers had increased from 50 to 400. Unfortunately, his health was failing rapidly due to a deteriorating heart condition that had already become evident by the end of the war. Lee died in 1870.

He lost his family home at Arlington, Virginia when the property was turned into a burial ground for soldiers, known today as Arlington National Cemetery. But in the years following his death, Lee's star rose and he became a widely revered figure among those outside the Southern gentry class. By the 1900s he had even become a respected figure in the North due to his reputation gallantry, gentlemanly conduct, and brilliant tactical successes. His U.S. Citizenship was restored posthumously by President Gerald Ford in 1975.

Robert E. Lee is an admired American figure both despite and because of his leadership of the Confederacy's forces during the Civil War. He was respected as a man of honor by his troops, adversaries, and his countrymen. He understood the importance of proper engineering and proper supply lines in war. He was able to inspire his troops to persevere even when they were hopelessly outnumbered.

Theories concerning his eventual failure abound among military historians. Did he depend too much on his subordinates? Was he too willing to put his men into harm's way? It may be difficult to arrive at a definitive answer. But as a general, perhaps his greatest success came in the years after the Civil War. He converted the raw emotion in the

South over the Confederacy's loss into a push to bind up the wounds in the United States and unite the North and South once again into an indissoluble union.

Perhaps it is Gerald Ford who best summarized Lee's character as he restored his citizenship:

"He sought to show by example that the citizens of the South must dedicate their efforts to rebuilding that region of the country as a strong and vital part of the American Union. As a soldier, General Lee left his mark on military strategy. As a man, he stood as the symbol of valor and of duty. As an educator, he appealed to reason and learning to achieve understanding and to build a stronger nation. The course he chose after the war became a symbol to all those who had marched with him in the bitter years towards Appomattox. General Lee's character has been an example to succeeding generations, making the restoration of his citizenship an event in which every American can take pride."

Conclusion

Battle Strategy Lessons From the Past for the 21st Century

Who is the greatest military leader in all of history? How is such a metric determined? Furthermore, can generals that lived two thousand years ago and conquered empires by the edge of a spear and phalanx unit offer wisdom to 21st century generals that conquer by pilotless drones, aircraft carriers, and Hellfire missiles?

This question was a major one in the nineteenth century (sans the Hellfire missiles), when European colonies engulfed the globe and the greatest empires held landed domains that were even greater than the Roman or Macedonian Empires. Authors crafted the "Great Captains" genre, which assessed the greatest military leaders in world history – all of those under consideration in this book and a few others, such as Saladin and George Washington – and determined lessons that could apply to their contemporary successors. Victor Davis Hanson commented that such handbooks theorized that human nature remained constant across space and time, and therefore whatever vast differences existed between spears and bullets was inconsequential compared to the human commonality of fear, calm, courage, and timidity, and how a universal military mind sizes up an enemy in any age.

Military historian Barry Strauss set out to answer this question of history's greatest general in his 2013 book "Master of Command: Alexander, Hannibal, Caesar, and the Genius of Leadership." He compared the qualities of the aforementioned generals according to three levels of criteria. First, they adroitly marshaled and directed armies; second, they used them for optimal strategic effect; third, they transformed these military victories into political power. He then compared these three generals according to the five stages that follow the course of war: "attack," or designing a plan for war; "resistance," or adapting and reacting to the enemy's pushback; "clash," or achieving victory over an enemy on the battlefield; "closing the net," or converting battlefield success into strategic victory; and "knowing when to stop" or transforming a successfully war into lasting peace.

According to this schema, Hannibal was the most brilliant battlefield tactician. He is a worthy candidate for such an honor. As we saw earlier in this book, his triumph at Cannae, in which he achieved double encirclement by a smaller army against a larger enemy, was repeated only a millennium later by Khalid ibn al-Walid. Alexander was the pre-eminent mobilizer of manpower and mobilization. He could harness unlimited money and manpower and convert his cult of celebrity into a massively devoted fighting force. Caesar, above all, transferred his victories into long-term strategic success and laid the foundations of the Roman Empire's power and stability. He was the patron saint of statesman.

The lessons for today's military generals from the past are, pardon the pun, legion; but perhaps the most applicable lessons for today derive from the final stages in war: closing the net and knowing when to stop. The major battles of the 21st century, such as the 2002 toppling of the Taliban and the 2003 U.S. Invasion of Iraq did very little to tax the military might of the American armed forces. The juggernaut rolled over the under-equipped Iraqi and Taliban armies in a matter of weeks. Furthermore, Western armies have no problems organizing and funding soldiers to fight in the most far-flung and inhospitable locations on earth.

The far more difficult task is to find a high-ranking general who can also act the statesman and turn a war-torn country whose leadership has been destroyed into a modern state. The military quagmire in Afghanistan for the last decade and the slow-boiling violence of Iraq are a testimony of the difficulty of brining a tidy end to a violent war. The U.S. bombings of Libya in 2011 or the much-discussed 2013 intervention in the Syrian civil war translate poorly into a moderate constitutional democracy with a thriving middle class. Perhaps that is what makes so remarkable such generals as David Petraeus, who took over the U.S. troop command of Iraq in 2007 during the height of its insurgency, when it was on the brink of a full civil war, and leaving behind a stabilizing country that is still mired in chaos but at least has become moderately functional.

Perhaps this is the greatest legacy that a military general can leave behind – that he is in fact not a general but a diplomat. Angelo Codevilla of Boston University has explained that diplomacy and military force are both means to the end of statecraft. A successful military campaign led by a brilliant tactician with well-trained soldiers and impressive weaponry at his disposal may create realities, but diplomacy represents them. War is not an end unto itself – except for the truly masochistic, none of which are under serious discussion in this book – but the means through which a leader achieves one's preferred peace. True, that peace may involve the subjugation, slaughter, or slavery of the dominated group underneath the boot of the conquerors. But this peace is no true peace at all, and a great general understands that his conquests will come to naught if the state he leaves behind in his wake crumbles as fast as the enemies' armies over which he ran roughshod.

Diplomacy, therefore is not about mutual good-faith or searching for agreements. It is not about tricking or lying to an opponent, but representing reality in precise words and warning the interlocutor, not threatening them. In such negotiations, the diplomat answers the question of "what are we after, and what are they after?" This question arrives at the heart of a civilization and reveals its most deep and treasured values. These negotiations determine what type of peace is sought and what type of peace the diplomat believes the other side seeks. Khalid, therefore, set out peace terms to conquered enemies by offering them three choices: abandon your city, convert to Islam, or pay a poll tax required by all non-Muslims. He was seeking to construct an entire Muslim social order that allowed for other beliefs, but placed Islam at the top of the ideological pyramid. This was the world he desired to live in, and he used war and diplomacy to achieve this end.

His social order existed relatively undisturbed, until over 1,000 years later when Napoleon invaded Egypt and signaled the beginning of European colonialism of the Middle East, which would upend the Muslim social order as well, creating a more Euro-centric one in its stead. As can been see, the limits set on pursuit of victory are limits on the commitment to each side for peace. Almost nobody ever fights to the last man and absolutely rules out surrender. Even the Mongols would surrender in defeat when they noticed that the enemy spared captives.

Perhaps it can be said that the greatest of all generals are those who avoid armed conflict altogether. They overawe the enemy to lay down arms out of fear before the first shot is fired or they reach a political solution that makes war unnecessary. As Sun Tzu commented 2,500 years ago during the war-torn Zhou Dynasty, no nation benefits from long-term warfare:

"For to win one hundred victories in one hundred battles is not the acme of skill. To subdue the enemy without fighting is the acme of skill."

Also by Michael Rank

The Crusades and the Soldiers of the Cross: The 10 Most Important Crusaders, From German Emperors to Charismatic Hermits, Child Armies, and Warrior Lepers

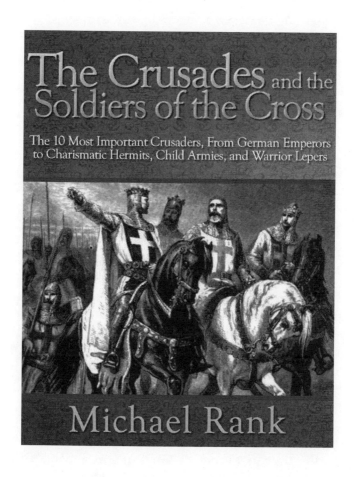

Turn the page to read an excerpt

Chapter 1

Peter the Hermit (1050-1115): The People's Preacher Who Resembled his Donkey

In 1092, three years before the first crusade, a Frankish pilgrim stood before the gates of Jerusalem and reluctantly paid the heavy toll to enter the city. He did not appear as if he had a gold coin in his possession – the man was short, thin, bore the coarse face of an ascetic, and wore the extremely rough material of a hermit. He was also dressed in the traditional garb of a pilgrim to Palestine: a scarf, wallet, and staff blessed by his parish priest before undertaking the trip. But he paid the toll to the Muslim sentinel and entered with his band of European pilgrims. However, half of those in his group could not afford this price, which equaled five Spanish dollars and was essentially price-gouging. They were prevented from finishing their pilgrimage, which they had spent months undertaking. As he entered the holy city, he witnessed other forms of exploitation on the pilgrims, such as being forced to pay entrance into the Redeemer's Tomb.

This and other instances of Muslim acts against Christian pilgrims aroused Peter to take up action. He used his two assets – enthusiasm and rousing oratory – and returned to Europe to assemble his own crusade alongside that of Urban II. He would assemble a rag-tag collection of peasants, low-ranking knights, and the elderly to liberate Jerusalem. They set out months before the official crusade, and their crusade was never planned or formally sanctioned by the Catholic Church. He would lead thousands across Europe and to the walls of Constantinople without any proper planning and without raising the necessary funds for such a trip. And Peter would also lead them to their slaughter at the hands of the experienced army of Seljuk commander Kilij Arslan.

There are a number of questions that surround Peter the Hermit, particularly around his involvement in instigating the First Crusade. Some claim that he was the main instigator, while others state that his involvement was overstated by earlier commentators. Since many of the facts about him come from his own preaching, which was often wildly embellished, it is not even known for sure if the above story about his trip to the Holy Land is true. What is not in dispute is that he was a charismatic preacher who helped organize and lead the People's Crusade, the name for his collection of peasants that set off even before the much more organized First Crusade was ready to embark on its voyage to the Holy Land.

His early life is surrounded by legend. Most scholars believe he was born around 1050 in the French town of Amiens, and lived the life of a hermit for a number of years (hence the name), embracing strict asceticism. He followed the example of Simeon (d. 451), who, according to tradition, spent 30 years on a pillar in order to recluse himself from the sinful world. He was short, unwashed, skinny, barefoot, and rode a donkey – the most humble of all means of conveyance, and an animal which many observers said resembled his rider. He refused to eat meat and bread, instead opting for fish and wine. Peter was said to have received a vision from Jesus Christ demanding that he approach Pope Urban II and request authority to preach the crusade. According to this legend, Pope Urban II not only gave Peter the Hermit the necessary authorization, but was also motivated to preach the crusade himself, which resulted in Urban II's speech calling for a crusade at the Council of Clermont. William of Tyre reported that, although Peter did approach Pope Urban II about gaining the authority to preach the crusade, there was no divine intervention in Peter's decision to approach the Pope. Although that does not mean he was not willing to claim divine intervention in other circumstances. Peter claimed that he received a letter from God that came down from heaven giving him authority to lead a crusade. He showed it to the crowds, which, due to their lack of literacy, could not dispute its authenticity.

His oratorical abilities were persuasive enough to convince peasants, many of whom had no military training nor geographical knowledge outside of their lord's estates, to give their lives to fighting against battle-hardened soldiers and capture a city on another continent. He admonished the crowds that their humble nature was a sign of their reliance on God and not a liability, but actually an asset. This was in contrast to Urban II's nobility and their reliance on planning and military experience. Conversely, Peter's peasants would have no other strength but the Lord, much like ancient Israel and its conquest of stronger enemies against all odds. Peter wandered through France preaching to ecstatic crowds, exhorting them to take up arms and free the Holy Land from the Muslims. He garnered respect from peasants and nobles alike, and would often give speeches in which the listeners were brought to tears. He was such a good speaker that, when Peter gave a speech in Germany, in a language that none of his listeners understood, people were still reduced to tears. His message to the populace of Muslim savagery and the imminent return of Christ was more apocalyptic than Urban II's message of penance and the cross.

Peter motivated thousands of people to join in the Crusades – something that Urban most definitely did not request of the hermit – and they set off on the pilgrimage route to Jerusalem much quicker that the Crusades being organized by the pope. This is exactly what the pope feared. Urban specifically mentioned in his speech at Clermont that "we do not command or advise that the old or feeble, or those unfit for bearing arms, undertake this journey; nor ought women to set out at all, without their husbands or brothers or legal guardians. For such are more of a hindrance than aid, more of a burden than advantage." Unfortunately, that was a perfect description of Peter's army. They did not have enough experience; many were in poor health, and joined for reasons of either intense piety or escaping the flood and pestilence of 1094 and famine in 1095. Being an agricultural worker in such circumstances made participating in a cause in which the opportunity to travel to a land flowing with milk and honey was quite promising.

However, there were not only commoners on his side.

Peter was also able to convince a number of lesser knights to join his cause, such as Walter Sans Avoir, who formed his own infantry corps that numbered a few thousand men. They acted as an advanced guard and led the army of 30,000 on the traditional pilgrimage route that followed the Rhine and Danube rivers. The lesser knights rode on horses, Peter rode on his donkey, and most of the peasants walked due to their poverty. Their line of march was over a mile long.

The Peasant's Crusade was not one mass group, but five different armies, the first of which was under the control of Peter. Although the peasant Crusaders were not kept under as tight of control as the forces under the command of Pope Urban II's noble princes, he kept his own forces from pillaging the countryside and villages along the pilgrimage route, at least in the early stages of the march. Unfortunately, the four armies that followed Peter were not as disciplined, and they ended up massacring a number of Jews during pogroms in Central Europe. Although Peter's forces were not involved in the pogroms, he still threatened and extorted funds for his crusade from Jews in the city of Trier, as well as other places. He showed the Jewish community in Trier a letter supposedly written by French Jews requesting that the Jewish community provide him with the necessary funds and supplies.

Peter set out with his followers in April of 1096 from Cologne, following in the wake of Walter Sans Avoir's army. Leaving at this time of year was exceptionally poor planning on Peter's part, and this decision would ultimately ruin their crusade in the months to come. Spring and summer were the hungry months in the Middle Ages, since the autumn harvest had not arrived, and subjects still subsisted on what was left in their winter storehouses. Therefore, they did not have much food to give or sell to the army. New crops were not yet ready. This is the reason Urban II told the main crusading force not to leave Europe until fall 1096, and this was the reason that pillaging, violence, and theft of food from villagers to avert starvation would come to define the People's Crusade.

From the early days of the march, it became clear that the

crowds would not listen to Peter, and they quickly give way to violence, looting, and pillaging if the opportunity presented itself. On May 23, 1096, Peter's followers arrived at Regensberg, where they forced the city's Jews to undergo a baptism before continuing on towards Constantinople. Sixteen of Walter's troops attempted to rob a market in the Hungarian town of Semlin when few provisions were made available. Officials captured them and humiliated them by hanging their clothes in front of the town as punishment. They had to proceed naked to Belgrade as a warning to anyone else who would try to rob a town of its limited food supply. The message was not heeded, and three weeks later, Peter's forces arrived at Semlin. While there, the Crusaders became suspicious of the fate of Walter Sans Avoir as a result of seeing sixteen suits of armor hanging from the walls. With suspicions running high, a dispute over the price of a pair of shoes exploded into a full-on riot with Peter's forces attacking and sacking the town, killing 4,000 and raiding Semlin's storehouse, leaving its inhabitants to face starvation.

The Byzantine Greeks soon became concerned about Peter's forces as the Peasant's Crusade continued toward Constantinople. They did not expect a full crusade to arrive until autumn. But when the crowd arrived at Nish on June 27 (and word soon followed of their sacking of Semlin), the Byzantine governor, Nicetas, agreed to allow Peter's followers access to markets in return for hostages that would be kept as collateral to prevent any potential violence. Peace was not kept for long, however, as Peter's followers once again began to riot. He tried to restore order but, when he was unable to do so, the Byzantine armies attacked and scattered Peter's forces. These battles cost Peter almost a third of his followers.

When the remaining Crusaders arrived at Sofia, they were met by a representatives of the Byzantine emperor, Alexius I. They hurried the Crusaders towards Constantinople and would not let the army remain in any place for more than three days to prevent another massacre. Peter's army was also given supplies by the Byzantine emperor. Once the Crusaders arrived at Constantinople, Alexius recommended that Peter wait until the First Crusade arrived. He did so, but also received news from messengers that few of the other contingents of Peasant's Crusade would join them. The rest, unable to support themselves, either starved or returned home. A large number were also captured and sold into slavery.

Peter united with Walter the Penniless, the leader of the other crusader group to successfully arrive at the Byzantine capital city, and the two groups combined into one large force. Peter then began to negotiate with Alexius for supplies and the means to be shipped across the Bosphorus strait into Turkish territory. Negotiations were completed, and Peter's followers were transported in early August. Alexius was hesitant to transport them into enemy territory and face an almost certain massacre, but he also knew that if the crowd remained close to Constantinople too long then his city was in danger. There had already been reports of robberies, lootings, and rapes against his Greek subjects in the city's suburbs.

Once across, disaster struck the Crusaders. Once the Peasant Crusade entered Turkish territory, they began to raid various villages and towns as they ventured through Anatolia. Once the Crusaders reached Nicomedia, Peter's forces broke into two factions, mostly along national lines, due to infighting. The two groups were composed of Germans and Italians in one group and French Crusaders in the other group. Both sides elected new leaders, with Rainaid taking control of the German/Italian group and Geoffrey Burel taking command of the French group. Once these new leaders were elected, Peter no longer had any control over the crusade or the peasants.

As the pilgrims continued to attack Turkish villages, the Seljuk Turks responded and prepared for a proper counterattack. Under the command of Kilij Arslan, the better trained Seljuk army put thousands of peasants to the sword in a series of battles, particularly when they were ambushed on the way to Nicea. The Peasant Crusaders were, for the most part, unarmed followers who had little experience with war and the better-disciplined Turkish soldiers made easy work of defeating them. Most of the pilgrims ended up either being killed or sold into slavery.

Peter escaped the catastrophe because he had travelled back to Constantinople to ask for military and provisional assistance, but the Byzantine Emperor was in no mood to provide any. As a result, Peter had nothing left to do but to wait for the better armed Crusaders from the First Crusade to arrive at Constantinople.

Remarkably, his story does not end there. The hermit did not exhibit any remorse about leading tens of thousands to their unnecessary deaths, as he still believed that God led him to assemble the People's Crusade, although he did not understand the divine purpose for them meeting such an ignominious end. His army was wiped out, but Peter's work with the Crusades continued onward. He realized that he lacked the abilities to lead an army, but also knew where his true strengths lied. Peter's inexhaustible enthusiasm would soon be directed to the next wave of Crusaders in the form of preaching and exhorting the troops to remain vigilant in their holy cause. According to Guibert of Nogent, Peter was present at the siege of Antioch, where the armed Crusaders were almost wiped out by the superior Turkish forces. Guibert states that Peter tried to escape from the city but Guibert also gives credit to Peter for the speech that encouraged the almost beaten Crusaders to counterattack and defeat the besieging Muslims. He also preached a sermon to the Crusaders at the Mountain of Olives before their final assault on Jerusalem, and rallied the troops to complete the act that they had labored toward for three hard years. Here is an example of Peter's true contribution to the Crusade: enthusiasm in the face of insurmountable odds. If it were not for figures such as him that had such unbounded optimism at the eventual success of their mission, then the soldiers would likely not have completed such a difficult task against all expectation.

Following the conquest of Jerusalem, Peter returned to Europe and lived another three decades. Little is known about his life events following the crusades, although it is recorded that he founded an Augustinian monastery in Neufmoustier, filled with relics from the Holy Land where many traveled to receive their blessings. Peter the Hermit died July 8, 1115. It is unknown if he was ever repentant about leading thousands of impassioned peasants to their slaughter, but his unreserved belief in the Crusade to capture Jerusalem was never in doubt.

End of this excerpt.

Enjoyed the preview?

BUY ON AMAZON TODAY

Connect With Michael

I hope you have enjoyed this e-book and learned much about the reigns of the most insane rulers in history.

You can connect with me on my homepage at http://michaelrank.net. Here you can find podcasts, blog posts, and other bits about history.

About the Author

Michael Rank is a doctoral candidate in Middle East history. He has studied Turkish, Arabic, Persian, Armenian, and French but can still pull out a backwater Midwestern accent if need be. He also worked as a journalist in Istanbul for nearly a decade and reported on religion and human rights.

He is the author of the #1 Amazon best-seller "From Muhammed to Burj Khalifa: A Crash Course in 2,000 Years of Middle East History," and "History's Worst Dictators: A Short Guide to the Most Brutal Leaders, From Emperor Nero to Ivan the Terrible."

One Last Thing

If you enjoyed this book, I would be grateful if you leave a review on Amazon. Your feedback allows me to improve current and future projects.

To leave a review please go to the book's Amazon page. Thank you again for your support!

Made in the USA
San Bernardino, CA
09 December 2013